D1168626

The Arts and Religion

246
B

Bailey, Albert E.

Loren Strait
Stockbridge
Mrs. Louis Bourne
3125 General Motors Rd.
Milford, Mich.
4/10
11/27/50 Ann....

2/3

4/22/47

May 14, 47
11/27/50
9/29/52

# THE ARTS AND RELIGION

THE MACMILLAN COMPANY
NEW YORK · BOSTON · CHICAGO · DALLAS
ATLANTA · SAN FRANCISCO

MACMILLAN AND CO., LIMITED
LONDON · BOMBAY · CALCUTTA · MADRAS
MELBOURNE

THE MACMILLAN COMPANY
OF CANADA, LIMITED
TORONTO

INTERIOR VIEW OF THE DESTROYED MONASTERY CHURCH OF CLUNY, 1088–1120 AND LATER

The largest, most highly evolved, and boldest Romanesque building. Except for the ineffective clearstory, it approximated Gothic effects, but it did not have true Gothic structure. (Wright model; photograph by Miss Elizabeth Sunderland; Conant drawing)

# THE
# ARTS AND RELIGION

*The Ayer Lectures of the*
*Colgate-Rochester Divinity School*
*1943*

*By*

ALBERT EDWARD BAILEY, *Editor*
KENNETH JOHN CONANT
HENRY AUGUSTINE SMITH
FRED EASTMAN

*New York*
THE MACMILLAN COMPANY
1944

A WARTIME BOOK

THIS COMPLETE EDITION IS PRODUCED IN FULL COMPLIANCE WITH THE GOVERNMENT'S REGULATIONS FOR CONSERVING PAPER AND OTHER ESSENTIAL MATERIALS

PRINTED IN THE UNITED STATES OF AMERICA

To the Memory of

# ALBERT WILLIAM BEAVEN

*Late President of the Colgate-Rochester
Divinity School*

# THE AYER LECTURES

*of the*

## COLGATE-ROCHESTER DIVINITY SCHOOL

### Rochester, N. Y.

The Ayer Lectureship was founded in May 1928, in the Rochester Theological Seminary by the gift of $25,000 from Mr. and Mrs. Wilfred W. Fry, of Camden, New Jersey, to perpetuate the memory of Mrs. Fry's father, the late Mr. Francis Wayland Ayer. At the time of his death, Mr. Ayer was president of the corporation which maintained the Rochester Theological Seminary.

Shortly after the establishment of the lectureship, the Rochester Theological Seminary and the Colgate Theological Seminary were united under the name of the Colgate-Rochester Divinity School. It is under the auspices of this institution that the Ayer lectures are given.

Under the terms of the foundation, the lectures are to fall within the broad field of the history or interpretation of the Christian religion and message. It is the desire of those connected with the establishment and the administration of the lectureship that the lectures shall be religiously constructive, and shall help in the building of Christian faith.

Four lectures are to be given each year at the Colgate-Rochester Divinity School at Rochester, New York, and these lectures are to be published in book form within one year after the time of their delivery. They will be known as the Ayer Lectures.

# Contents

|  |  | PAGE |
|---|---|---|
| INTRODUCTION: The Antiquity and Universality of the Arts. *Albert Edward Bailey* | | 3 |
| I. | The Expression of Religion in Painting and Sculpture. *Professor Bailey* | 35 |
| II. | The Expression of Religion in Architecture. *Kenneth John Conant* | 71 |
| III. | The Expression of Religion in Music. *H. Augustine Smith* | 93 |
| IV. | The Dramatist and the Minister. *Fred Eastman* | 135 |
| Index | | 171 |

# *Illustrations*

PLATE                                                    OPP. PAGE

&ast; Interior View of the Destroyed Monastery
Church of Cluny, 1088–1120 and later. *Frontispiece*

I. The Weighing of the Soul
From the Papyrus of Hunefer, British Museum,
c.1500 B.C.                                                    10

II.A. Théobald Chartran: St. Francis Singing,
19th century                                                  11

B. The Taj Mahal, Agra, India, Mohammedan,
17th century

III.A. Jain Temple of Neminath, Mt. Abu, India,
11th century                                                  16

B. Temple of Horus, Edfu, Egypt, 3rd century
B.C.

IV.A. Court and Sanctuary, Mosque of Sultan
Hasan, Cairo, 14th century                                    17

B. Nave of Exeter Cathedral, England, 13th
century

V.A. Solar Emblems. Tomb of Ramses III, Valley
of the Kings, Egypt, 12th century B.C.                        38

B. Siva Dancing. From south India, 15th century

VI.A. Athena Assisting Herakles, Metope of Zeus
Temple, Olympia, Greece, 5th century B.C.                     39

B. Michelangelo: God Creating Adam. Sistine
Chapel, Rome, 1512 A.D.

VII.A. Sculptured Rail, Sanchi, India. Buddhist,
5–3rd century B.C.                                             44

xi

PLATE                                                    OPP. PAGE

B. Frescoes of SS. Peter and Paul. Catacomb in
Rome, Early 3rd century

VIII.A. Greek Vase Painting: Herakles Captures
Cerberus, 6th century B.C.                          45

B. Christ Raises Lazarus. Karlsruhe Gospels,
Romanesque, c. 1150 A.D.

IX.A. The Last Judgement. Sculptured lintel from
Bourges Cathedral, France, 13th century          50

B. Three Worthies in the Furnace. Christian
Sarcophagus, Rome, 4th century

X.A. Fra Angelico: The Crucifixion (detail). San
Marco monastery, Florence, Italy, 1443 A.D.      51

B. Parable of the Two Houses. Reformation
cartoon, Germany, 16th century

XI.A. Merson: Fra Angelico Painting, 19th century     58

B. The Dormition of the Virgin. Window in
Chartres Cathedral, France, 13th century

XII. Chinese Painting: White Eagle and Pine Tree       59

XIII.A. Thomas Benton: Again                             64

B. Orozco: Homecoming of the Workers in the
New Day

XIV. Three Frescoes by Quinquela Martin                65
A. Unloading Coal
B. Departure of Fishermen
C. Self-Portrait

XV. Old St. Peter's, Rome, 4th century                 74
* A. Restored bird's-eye view
* B. Restored interior perspective
C. Restored plan

XVI. St. Sophia, Istanbul, 6th century                 75
* A. Restored east view, showing supposed original scheme

PLATE                                                    OPP. PAGE

  B. Reflected plan

 * C. Analytical section showing structural character

   acter

XVII. St. Sophia, Istanbul, 6th century and later

   Interior view made before secularization  80

XVIII. Carolingian Developments of Basilican Architecture

   tecture  81

 * A. Monastery of Centula, later called St. Riquier, 8th century

   quier, 8th century

  B. St. Philibert de Grandlieu, 9th century

  C. St. Germain, Auxerre. Crypt of 841–51 A.D.

XIX. Comparison of Archaic and Developed Romanesque

   manesque  84

 * A. St. Bénigne, Dijon, 1001–18 and later. Original plan

   inal plan

 * B. Santiago de Compostela, 1078–1140 and later. Original plan

   later. Original plan

XX. Comparison of Archaic and Developed Romanesque

   manesque  85

 * A. St. Bénigne, Dijon, 1001–18 and later. Original scheme

   inal scheme

 * B. Santiago de Compostela, 1078–1140 and later. Original scheme

   later. Original scheme

XXI. Reims Cathedral, 1211–85 and later  86

 * A. West view with addition of spires, planned but never built

   but never built

  B. Plan

  C. View of nave with stained glass removed

XXII. Beauvais Cathedral: The Sanctuary  87

XXIII. A. Youth Choirs, Second Presbyterian Church, Bloomington, Ill.

   Bloomington, Ill.  128

  B. Choral Arts Singers, Boston University

PLATE                                                      OPP. PAGE

XXIV. A. Scene in an Air Raid Shelter. From Dr. Eastman's play, *Eternal Life*          129
B. Scene from *Pageant of Worship*, First Congregational Church, Los Angeles

---

* Research project, here published for the first time

Introduction

# THE ANTIQUITY AND UNIVERSALITY
# OF THE ARTS

*By* Albert Edward Bailey

# THE ANTIQUITY AND UNIVERSALITY
## OF THE ARTS

ART HAS ITS ROOTS so deep in human nature that we are obliged to characterize it as an instinctive activity. Whatever specific forms the art impulse may take, its essence is to impose upon experience certain categories; to rearrange the data of life into patterns, to regulate, reject, emphasize, systematize, so that the re-created experience may yield to the spirit a fuller satisfaction than did the original one. When as a country boy on my way to school I passed a picket fence, the temptation was irresistible to hold a stick against the pickets in order to enforce through my ear the rhythm my eye had already discovered; and then to further enhance the joy by complicating the rhythm—by swinging my arm in long swoops that made the stick say "rat-a-tat-tat, rat-a-tat-tat." Such an act did the fence no good but it did me good; and later it helped me understand what Dr. William E. Hocking meant by his phrase, "necessary desires"—the desire to impose rhythm and other patterns upon experience. Among these necessary desires are unity, balance, proportion, harmony—whatever qualities the "Art-for-art's-sake" people claim to constitute the sum-total of art.

These necessary desires have appeared in all ages and in all races. An ivory figurine of a woman (the *Venus of Willendorf*) found in France and dating from the Aurignacian period, say, 25,000 B.C., denaturalizes the form by a rhythmic and balanced arrangement of masses. Another masterpiece found in a grotto of the Dordogne region and dating from Magdalenian times, perhaps 12,000 B.C., is a herd of grazing reindeer incised on the radius bone of an eagle's

3

wing. It shows a sophisticated manipulation and even gives an impressionistic suggestion rather than a delineation of form. These qualities that turn objects into works of art are to be seen in flints from widely scattered places; in the rhythmic arrangement and conventionalized forms of the rock paintings and engravings of South Africa, the Sahara Atlas, the Libyan desert, Spain, northern Italy, Scandinavia; and in date they range from 200,000 to 2,000 B.C. Moreover the art of primitive peoples, living today and as widely separated as the South African Bushman and the American Indian, shows identical characteristics. These facts would seem to confirm Dr. Hocking's assertion that the esthetic aspects of art are aboriginal.

Religion is also an instinctive phenomenon, if by religion we mean the urge of the soul to make helpful contact with unseen sources of power. It likewise is universal and aboriginal. The Mousterian-age graves in the caves of Mt. Carmel, 100,000 years old, show burials in the so-called "embryonic" position, which archaeologists interpret as an expectation that, through the generative powers of mother earth, man will be born again in another life. Excavators in the oldest mounds of Mesopotamia, Crete, Egypt, India, China, dig up gods, cult objects, the foundations of temples small and great; in the jungles of Yucatan they explore the wonders of Mayan pyramid-temples. All ancient literatures from all lands resound with prayers and hymns to the gods who hold the open sky or reside in spring or tree as fructifiers of earth. Go where you will, you hear the sky-born music still. As the spring sun sends its energy into the earth, and

> Every clod feels a stir of might,
> An instinct within it that reaches and towers,
> And, groping blindly above it for light,
> Climbs to a soul in grass and flowers,

so the dormant powers of man's soul respond to the all-compelling evolutionary urge and climb out of their prison-house to blossom in saints and prophets and saviours.

The tie-up between religion and the prehistoric arts of drawing, painting and sculpture came through magic, which was used to secure the possession of the desirable objects represented by the artist, and to compel the help of unseen powers. Cave paintings were made not primarily to be exhibited to an admiring crowd as works of art but were often to be used ritualistically in the darkest recesses of the grotto sometimes half a mile from the entrance. The formulas chanted in their presence by the hunters or the medicine-men were calculated to draw the animals represented within reach of spear or arrow and to make them vulnerable. Men are frequently shown performing ritual ceremonies, notably those that produce rain through the agency of the morning star, symbolized by a female figure which has survived into historic times as Venus; or the ceremonials have to do with burials. From such widely-scattered bits of evidence we understand that art and religion were partners from the start. They remained partners until in late historic times men found that art might serve other interests besides religion.

When men climbed out of pre-history and primitivism they brought their human equipment with them: they continued to be both religious and artistic. Learning the lessons taught by social experience, they humanized their gods, elevated them into the sky, gave them a conscience and socialized them. They imposed upon them the same types of organization they themselves had evolved. The gods became warriors, kings, fathers of their people, guarantors of justice, emperors with international sovereignty. The Egyptian pre-dynastic Set and Horus fought their personal and tribal feuds; but Amon of Thebes outgrew his provincial demesne, as did his earthly counterpart the Pharaoh, became the chief of a national pantheon, and finally lord of every land the Pharaonic arms conquered. The Israelite Yahweh ceased in time to be a god of storms, as unpredictable as they; he made covenants that bound both himself and his people to certain loyalties; he became the defender of justice, an exponent of pity and of redeeming grace. The Greek Zeus who began similarly as god of the clouds, the rain and the thunder, developed in the direction of a Greek "tyrant," and finally, in a pinch, descended from his autocracy to get suggestions from his council of the gods, much as at Athens the *archon basileus* was obliged periodically to get a vote of confidence from the Athenian assembly.

That is the noticeable thing about the gods: they persist in growing up. As Voltaire said, "God made man in his own image, and man returned the compliment."

Now art grows up also. After the magic-impregnated bison of Altamira comes finally the devotion-impregnated "Deposition" of Fra Angelico. Out of the "standing stones" of the Semites, phallic symbols of the Baals of fertility who sojourned in them, grew the Temple of Solomon in the thick darkness of which dwelt the God not made with hands; and finally arrived the great cathedral which is an instrument whereby man may effect a union of his finite self with the infinite source of power. Out of the primitive tom-toms by which the gods were summoned to the sacrificial feast, out of the shepherd's pipes and the processional chants of religion, came the lyre of David, the plainsong of Gregory, the polyphony of Palestrina, the Passion music of Bach, and the humble anthem sung by the country choirs of a thousand churches. Out of the religious ceremonies of the god Dionysus, with their dancing, singing and rough horse-play, came Greek tragedy; and out of it and its later brother, the miracle play of the medieval church, grew the Elizabethan drama and the contemporary plays of social criticism. The distinctive qualities of all the arts can be traced back to man's original endowment; in their present structures can be discerned the genes which have transmitted to them their hereditary fundamental characteristics.

## I

In the first lecture of this series devoted to the plastic arts I have tried to show specifically how religion has found a medium of expression in painting and sculpture; or to put it the other way round, how these two arts have been able to serve man's deepest needs by making visually concrete and intelligible the powers, persons, beliefs and values associated with religion. This is art looked at from the creative angle: impulse and desire finding satisfaction through expression; instinct translating itself into action. That is the tendency of all desires—to realize themselves. The life history of all artists is reflected in the lines from Longfellow's Kéramos:

> Thine was the prophet's vision, thine
> The exaltation, the divine
> Insanity of noble minds,
> That never falters nor abates,
> But labors and endures and waits,
> Till all that it foresees it finds,
> *Or what it cannot find creates!*

In this introductory essay I should like to approach religious art from another angle, from the receiving end. What does religious art do to us—to you and me who are not creators?

In the first place it can challenge us. It can make the great affirmation that religion is worth our attention and that art is an authentic expression of it.

In these days both these affirmations are doubted. It is smart to deny the claims of religion. A materialistic philosophy endeavoring to interpret a material universe has by-passed some of the most essential goods of humanity and has led this generation into cynicism and atheism. Santayana straddles the gulf between his philosophy and his Catholic inheritance by saying, "There is no God, and Mary is His mother"! Contemporary artists also assert that there is no God by refusing to have anything to do with him and by painting for a Madonna any pretty girl with a baby. In any modern exhibition of art the religious subjects can be counted on the fingers of one hand. The proper subjects for art today are bananas and triangles, or triangles without the bananas; one-eyed or three-eyed women flattened by a steam roller and hung up to dry; distortions, fragmentations, montages, Freudian nightmares in which a horsefly on a plate is Salvador Dali's reminiscence of father. The modern *isms* of art belong really in the category of technical experiments: through them the artist is feeling his way to a more pungent mode of expression. But unless he has something to express, what is the use? I have often envied a dragoman I used to hire in Smyrna: he could speak eighteen languages. But he had nothing to say in any one of them!

The great art of the past brings us up short. Why did those geniuses of old paint religious pictures? Did they themselves discover in life something transcendent? Or if they were merely technicians, did the men who commissioned them to paint feel that the affirmations of faith were worth the price they had to pay? Why must God stare at us out of a fifth-century mosaic and a seventeenth-century El Greco and a twentieth-century Sargent? Is it because the human heart for these fifteen hundred years has needed him? Somehow God will not down. We give him the high-hat in our philosophy, we annihilate him with our science, but he comes back like a wraith; he pursues us like the Hound of Heaven.

> They reckon ill who leave me out;
> When me they fly, I am the wings;
> I am the doubter and the doubt,
> And I the hymn the Brahmin sings.

Art through the ages is witness to the inescapability of God. And if he has proved to be inescapable, we would better give him attention.

But is this art an authentic expression of religion? We can answer that question only by the pragmatic test: we can endeavor to recover the artist's original experience by the process of sympathetic penetration and then say whether the ideas and the emotions aroused in us have the ring of genuineness.

The technique of this testing is easy to acquire. It has two phases, an intellectual and an emotional. Approaching a work of art from the former viewpoint we try to find out exactly what the artist is saying. Is this a story-telling picture? In that case who are the persons, what are the human relationships exhibited; is the time-sequence of the story clear; do action, facial expression, fit the theme and the moment; is the total impression consonant with the idea that gives the story significance? We might even ask ourselves whether the significance itself is valuable; whether the story reveals through its persons and action those attitudes toward life that make living more dignified, more humane, more altruistic; whether it moves in the direction we all in our better moments desire to go. All this is an attempt at intellectual appraisal of the content, not of the technique. If we can say yes to these questions we shall have to admit that the artist has made a contribution to our understanding of life's values. If religion has any value, it also must point in the same direction.

Or suppose the theme of the picture is dogmatic—do you understand what the dogma is? Can you state it in words? Do the persons in the picture show by posture and emotion that they accept or incarnate this truth or are essential to the exposition of it? It may be an outmoded dogma, one that you personally cannot accept. But recalling that men did once accept it, that men have given their lives in defense of it, that it was once part and parcel of a civilization built upon it, then can you tell whether, granted the medieval point of view, the artist has clarified the meaning, taught it skillfully, forcefully? You might go even further and ask yourself whether that medieval concept can be translated from theological into humanistic or even scientific terms, and so be utilized by us moderns in our endeavor to understand and enhance life.

To illustrate: take the "Weighing of the Soul" from the Papyrus of Hunefer, 1500 B.C. (Plate I). Here in attendance are the hybrid gods of Egypt; the balances that hold Hunefer's heart in one pan and the hieroglyphic for "Truth" in the other; the dread Eater of the Dead crouching to devour the heart if it does not meet the test; Osiris and the other enthroned deities waiting to welcome Hunefer if he is successful; and the candidate himself watching the process with evident trepidation. Of course that picture represents nothing factual: souls do not get weighed in that fashion. But do they get judged? Did Giotto have anything valid to say on this subject in the Padua chapel? Did Michelangelo enshrine only a myth in his Sistine "Last Judgement"? Did Sargent merely reminisce when he returned to the scales imagery in the Boston Public Library? Was the Scripture too in error when it announced "Whatsoever a man soweth, that shall he also reap"? Was William James fooling when he wrote in his *Psychology* that famous passage about Rip's excuse for drinking ("This time won't count"):

Well! He may not count it, and a kind heaven may not count it; but it is being counted none the less. Down among the nerve cells and fibers the molecules are counting it, registering it and

## PLATE I

### THE WEIGHING OF THE SOUL

From the Papyrus of Hunefer, British Museum (c. 1500 B.C.)

PLATE II (A)

ST. FRANCIS SINGING

By Théobald Chartran (nineteenth century)

PLATE II (B)

THE TAJ MAHAL, AGRA, INDIA

Mohammedan (seventeenth century)

storing it up to be used against him when the next temptation comes. Nothing we ever do is, in strict scientific literalness, wiped out.

When you let your mind loose upon a work of art, you may discover that the masterpiece has something to say to you; that in spite of an old-fashioned dress and an alien face there is a kernel of idea inside it which is alive and importunate and true.

In this way you find that the picture is doing to yourself the very thing it did to the artist's contemporaries of long ago. The artist has put his message "into a form that is not abolished by the passing of time."

Let us now consider the emotional approach to a work of art.

In all art, feeling is primary whether as a dynamic of creation or as a mode of appreciation. No masterpiece can be born out of cold intellectuality; without fire there is no warmth, no urge. To represent the great human values of joy, courage, faith, love, self-sacrifice, the artist must first feel them and out of that feeling generate the will to give them plastic form. Then through painstaking observation he must discover how persons in the grip of those emotions betray that fact to the world: he must become psychologist and anatomist. Finally, in his imagery he imprisons these emotions through his skill in rendering spiritual states. These emotions are waiting for you to release them.

Here you stand in the presence of this inanimate canvas— let us imagine it is Chartran's *St. Francis Singing* (Plate II A). Can you make these dead bones live? Yes. As St. Francis first felt and then gave his emotion a bodily expression, so you can reverse the process. Get inside the good saint. Throw your weight upon the plow handles, push with your feet; cast your eye up to the sun which brings the promise of spring; sing your faith that beyond the plowing are the sowing and the reaping, that even though the mountain is barren and birds hover to snatch away the seed, God will not let seedtime and harvest fail. And as you thus manipulate your body, even if only in imagination, the feeling-correlate will appear in consciousness; you will know what the saint experienced in the way of joy in the midst of labor, hope in the midst of discouragement, confidence that the world was friendly:

Praised be my Lord God with all his creatures, and especially our brother the Sun, who brings us the light. And for our sister the Moon, and for the Stars. For our brother the Wind, and for Air and Cloud. For our sister Water. For our Mother the Earth.

That is the essence of this picture: the stubborn earth is forced to yield its harvest of joy to one who works in faith. You cannot prove that proposition to be true by any intellectual process, but you can feel it to be true for saints like Francis.

Never let a work of art go until you have wrung from it the blessing of emotion.

How persistently people try to absorb these values in art, both intellectual and emotional. And how patiently the picture waits century after century to be understood and loved. In 1895 I first entered the room in Dresden where is hung Raphael's *Sistine Madonna*. Before it a crowd of people were sitting in silence, eyes fastened upon that face which suggests the mystery of motherhood, the sense of participation with God in creation and salvation, and the inability of a mortal to comprehend a role so sublime. To understand such a picture is to have a religious experience.

I came again in 1908: there was the same room, the same picture; but a different throng sat in silence before it. Again I came in 1920: a new crowd. Again in 1927—but now a different generation of people were there, exposing themselves to the inspiration that for four hundred years had streamed from that canvas and will continue to shine down upon men until canvas and pigment are dust.

This is an illustration of the perpetual ministry of religious art to the human spirit.

## II

Architecture is several millenniums younger than painting and sculpture. It came into being not only after men ceased to live in caves but after they had acquired enough leisure and surplus wealth to build enduringly. Even then their structures were not architecture until those "necessary desires" began to modify their crudities, began to introduce symmetry, balance, proportion, rhythm, and to make them yield those spiritual satisfactions which Dr. Conant has so beautifully expressed in his lecture. Just when that esthetic emergence occurred we cannot say with certainty. Sir C. Leonard Woolley [1] has reported temple structures which exhibit the basic principles of architectural design and decoration at Warka, Kish and Erech in Mesopotamia, dating from the early fourth millennium B.C. These are perhaps the earliest so far found. In Egypt, monumental architecture in stone began with the terraced pyramid at Sakkara (III Dynasty, 28th century B.C.) with its complex of tombs and shrines; but these buildings were stone translations of earlier reed-and-mud, or mud-brick, structures.[2] In all the early survivals the buildings seem to have served religion: they were either temples or mortuary shrines. From these dates in the two earliest homes of civilization we have a continuing architectural tradition in the area of religion to the very present.

In considering this second topic of our series, our first inquiry should be the function of religious architecture: for what purposes were these structures built?

---

[1] Sir C. Leonard Woolley: *The Development of Sumerian Art,* 1935, Chap. I.
[2] James H. Breasted: *A History of Egypt,* 1912, Chap. V.

One of the earliest purposes was Remembrance. In the days when gods were limited in their habitations, if by chance a man had contact with deity in a particular spot, that place was worth remembering. Jacob fleeing his country and his father's god had a dream at Bethel, and on awakening exclaimed, "Surely the Lord is in this place and I knew it not." Accordingly he called the name of that place the "House of God" (Beth-el).[3] Thereafter he was always sure of finding God in that particular spot marked by his pillar.[4] It remained sacred, the site of a national sanctuary, for a thousand years until a jealous rival destroyed it.

At Abydos on the Nile, Osiris, Lord of the Resurrection, was buried. That place was marked by the grand temple of the Osireion, which was the center of Egyptian worship for 2500 years. The Parthenon at Athens was not only a home of the goddess Athena when she came to visit her favorite city, but a memorial of the victories over Persia won by her aid.

Other memories besides those about the gods are made permanent by architecture. At Mihintale in Ceylon a huge dagoba or stupa enshrines the luminous hair that grew on Buddha's forehead, and a smaller stupa marks the spot where King Asoka's son and missionary met and converted to the Buddhistic faith King Tissa (3rd century B.C.). At Agra, India, is that dream of beauty called the Taj Mahal (Plate II B). This was an emperor's offering to the memory of his favorite wife, the "Crown of the Palace," mother of thirteen of his children. It took the form of a mosque and was accompanied by two other mosques of red sandstone—dusky slaves that wait perpetually upon their mistress—because mosques are reminders that men must submit to the will of Allah, which is the essence of Islam. This memorial has therefore

---

[3] Gen. 28:10–22.
[4] Gen. 35:6–7.

a double inseparable reference: to God and to a greatly loved person now with Him in Paradise.

At Santiago de Compostela in Spain, focal point of pilgrimages for 500 years, the grand cathedral rises to commemorate St. James the Greater, patron of all pilgrims. St. Sophia at Constantinople is an imperial memorial to the doctrine of the Logos—Holy Wisdom as revealed in Christ. Sainte Chapelle in Paris is a Gothic reliquary for the Crown of Thorns; and most of the greater churches of Europe commemorate some saint, a relic of whom is treasured under the high altar. Men have not willingly let die the memory of great men and significant events, and monumental buildings are their most effective reminders.

But these structures often serve other purposes beside remembrance. As in Jacob's experience, the holy place became the House of God; and man's heart has ever been set to honor deity with the best dwelling place his skill could construct. That is why though human habitations perish with the years, God's house remains. The eternal gods must have eternal habitations. Even when the concept of the temple as dwelling place was outgrown, the name "God's House" persisted; and so did the idea that the best which man possesses should be offered to deity. Costliness presented to God in his sanctuary is an expression of the supreme value man places upon religion (Plate III A).

Since religion is not merely an individual matter but belongs to the family, the tribe, the community, the shrine must be adapted to communal worship. With the growth of villages into cities, the place of worship had to be enlarged. Increasing size and magnificence added dignity to the ceremonials there performed, symbolized the power and wealth of the commune or even the majesty of the empire. As Dr. Conant hints, such a building even served a worldly purpose: as when Constantine, convinced that religion was the only agency that could weld together and save his doubtful *imperium*, raised Christianity from underground, established it as the recognized faith of the State, and emphasized its universal significance by building for it the magnificent basilicas of the *Nativity* at Bethlehem, the *Martyrion* at Jerusalem, *Old St. Peter's* at Rome, the original *Holy Wisdom* and the enlarged *Holy Peace* at Constantinople—besides many others.

So far, then, we might say that religious architecture is the expression of certain fundamental human needs: the need to commemorate both gods and holy men, holy places and doctrines; the need to provide a dwelling place—actual or symbolic—that should be worthy of deity, large enough to serve a whole community or a state, and costly enough to demonstrate the supreme value of religion. But granted these primary satisfactions, the architect must consider also the special functions the building has to perform. Chief among these is adaptation to ritual.

When the temple was regarded literally as God's house, the architecture was assimilated to that of a palace, and the function was to facilitate the god's living in state. Take, for example, the temple of Horus at Edfu (Plate III B). The god dwelt in the thick darkness of his chamber toward the rear of the inner structure; in fact, his bed-chamber was a room cut from a single stone and fitted with bronze doors, behind which he had absolute privacy. This chamber was in the center of a larger room where were performed the offices of eating, being washed and dressed, consulted and entertained. Priests were his servants organized into a hierarchy, from the Major Domo or High Priest down to the menials. About this living room were a series of cubicles used as storage rooms where the god's clothes, regalia and treasure were stored. In front of these personal rooms were two antechambers where his servants stood guard; then the hypostyle

## PLATE III (A)

JAIN TEMPLE OF NEMINATH, MT. ABU, INDIA

(eleventh century)

## PLATE III (B)

TEMPLE OF HORUS, EDFU, EGYPT

(third century B.C.)

PLATE IV (A)

COURT AND SANCTUARY, MOSQUE OF SULTAN HASAN, CAIRO

(fourteenth century)

PLATE IV (B)

NAVE OF EXETER CATHEDRAL, ENGLAND

(thirteenth century)

hall which served as a Hall of Audience for representatives from other temples or a reception room for visiting divinities —as when, enthroned in state, Horus welcomed the goddess Hathor from Dendera as she paid a courtesy call. In front of this room lay the Grand Vestibule where the god's own dignitaries presented themselves for worship. Before the tall façade of the house was a court open to the sky and surrounded by a cloister. There on the feast days the processionals of the priests, priestesses and sacrificial animals deployed after marching through the town and around the cloisters and colonnades of the outer palace. Two lofty towers flanking the gate in the girdle wall gave notice from afar that here was the divine residence.

These general arrangements persisted with modification and disguise through many centuries. Christian churches still have their sacred inner places—the ciborium that contains the Real Presence, the tabernacle that guards the ciborium, the altar-table where offerings are made and mystic rites are performed, the chancel reserved for the assisting servants or ministers. There is the "sacred meal" at which communicants become partakers of divine food. The altar as well as the hierarchy is "dressed" with "vestments" brought from a near-by treasure room or sacristy. There are ambulatories and aisles and cloisters for processionals. Worshippers still bring "offerings," especially on festival days that commemorate incidents in the human life of God.

As the palace idea becomes more and more a metaphor, as the "service" becomes worship instead of work, and preaching is added as a technique for propaganda and inspiration, the temple suffers a sea-change: it becomes a church, the structure of which is calculated to create in the faithful the moods of worship, of inspiration, of self-dedication. The function, now performed by architecture, is to induce by its lines, masses, spaces, vistas, focal points, and colors, a sense of awe, of elevation, even of ecstasy; to provide the requisites for listening, the environment for meditation, and the feeling of companionship in worship (Plate IV A). This change in point of view and consequently in structure went on through many centuries and culminated in the European cathedrals of the thirteenth century (Plate IV B). Since that date religious architecture has remained stationary in its ideals though declining in its accomplishment because religion has lost its position of primacy.

In the second chapter of our book Dr. Conant has given us the case histories of certain churches which reflect the ideals of four successive periods and reveal a functional relationship to the religious demands of their age. These churches are Old St. Peter's in Rome built in the fourth century by Constantine; the church of Holy Wisdom (St. Sophia) built in Constantinople by Justinian in the sixth century; the North-European churches of the ninth to eleventh centuries exemplified by the imperial monastery of Centula (N. France), St. Bénigne (Dijon, E. France), and Santiago de Compostela (Spain); and the twelfth-century monastery church of Cluny (E. France), precursor of Chartres. In his succinct and cameo-like presentation you will be able not only to follow the changing influences of time, race, ritual and social organization, but to feel the spiritual contribution that great architecture perpetually makes to the religious life of man.

## III

Noise became music when man began to impose upon mere vibration the categories of his "necessary desires"— when he modified sound in the direction of rhythm, pattern, balance, structure. This modification is the work of intelligence and that is perhaps the reason why primitive tribes, though they make plenty of noise, have as little music as they have science or mathematics. Music comes last in the chronology of the arts.

Since, unlike the spacial arts, music leaves no physical trace behind, we cannot tell when man began to make it. The prehistoric caves yield no evidence. Well along the stream of historic time, however, the archaeologists turn up musical instruments. Instruments of percussion seem to be earliest, then flutes, then strings. This order would suggest that rhythm was the first modification to be imposed upon sound, followed by melody. Since early literary references invariably make music an adjunct of poetry and dancing, this fact would confirm the priority of rhythm over the other characteristics. Harmony was a late invention.

The earliest stringed instruments so far discovered come from the Sumerian royal cemetery of Al-Urbaid, and they are lyres made by skilled craftsmen. One of these has its sound-box decorated with a bull's head of thin sheet gold. Since the bull is provided with a beard of lapis lazuli set in a silver frame, Sir Leonard Woolley its discoverer concludes that these features had a ritualistic origin.[5] If this conjecture is correct, religion and music have now joined hands, in the fourth millennium B.C.

From this beginning, evidence multiplies that instrumental and vocal music have always been integral parts of religious services. In Egypt by the sixteenth century B.C. and no doubt earlier, the wife of the high priest was leader of the singing women who entertained the gods in their temples.[6] Hymns to the gods were part of all ritual.

In the Old Testament there is abundant testimony to the union of religion and music. After the deliverance of the Israelites at the Red Sea (c.1290 B.C.) Miriam and her women praised Yahweh with timbrel, dance and antiphonal

---

[5] C. Leonard Woolley: *The Development of Sumerian Art*, 1935, page 76.
[6] J. H. Breasted: *A History of Egypt*, 1912, page 248.

song.[7] The prophetess Deborah after her victory at the Kishon praised him with a paean of song.[8] The "ecstatic prophets" of Israel (1050–950 B.C.) used music to induce the hypnotic frenzy which was prerequisite to the divine revelation [9]— even as the whirling dervishes of Islam do today, or did until the Turkish organizations were dissolved by Moustapha Kemel. Amos tells indirectly that music was part of the organized ritual of Israelite shrines, 850 B.C.:

> I hate, I despise your feasts,
>     And I will take no delight in your solemn assembles.
>
> ·    ·    ·    ·    ·    ·    ·    ·
>
> Take thou away from me the noise of thy songs,
>     For I will not hear the melody of thy viols.[10]

And we know from the Books of Chronicles that elaborate choirs with voice and instruments were the great glory of the services in the Second Temple at Jerusalem, 516 B.C. to 70 A.D.

Greek mythology, which is a late imaginative explanation of very ancient beliefs, bears witness to the tie-up of music and religion. It tells us that the lyre was the invention of the gods Hermes, Athena and Apollo; that the Muses, who were the daughters of Zeus and Mnemosyne (Memory), bestowed upon men the gift of song, and Apollo himself furnished divine inspiration. The mother-goddess Cybele, imported very early into Greece from Asia Minor, was celebrated with orgiastic flute music. A myth tells how flute-playing Marsyas, a priest of Cybele, challenged the lyre-playing Apollo to a musical contest, was defeated and flayed alive for his presumption—a Greek way of saying that flutes

---

[7] Ex. 15:21.
[8] Jdg. 5:3.
[9] 1 Sam. 10:5–6; 2 Kgs. 3:14–16.
[10] Amos 5:21–23.

belong to primitive men and religions, while the lyre is the instrument of civilization and the Olympian gods.

In its origin, Christian music was vocal and unaccompanied. The earliest song of Christ's followers was the Jewish "Hallel," [11] sung at the Last Supper.[12] Ever since that Upper Room gathering, song has been the unfailing expression of the Christian's faith and hope and love—indeed, it was the differentiating feature of early Christian meetings, as Pliny reported in his letter to the emperor Trajan, c.112 A.D. The Christians "sang a song to Christ as to a God." [13] People usually sing their joy; and the joys that arise in the heart over the consciousness of sins forgiven, the promise of heaven, devotion to the Saviour, the brotherhood of all men of good will, are deep-seated and contagious. The vitality of religion in any given epoch may be accurately gauged by the vigor of communal song; and, in reverse, when the people cease to sing and the choirs and the organ take over, understand that religion has waned.

Missionary epochs are singing epochs; reform eras are passionately songful. Luther's Reformation was a popular revolt not only against a corrupt church but against the economic oppressions and the suppression of the free life of the thirteenth-century communes and artisans' guilds by the growing autocracies of kings and plutocrats, a revolt against the loss of those dreams of human brotherhood that had once seemed destined to be fulfilled. When Luther revived those hopes and championed the people's cause, song burst forth—folktunes set to fighting words like "Ein feste Burg"—and the Reformation rolled forward triumphantly. But later when Luther sought political alliances with the autocratic princes to help him overcome the armed opposition of Holy Church,

---

11 Psalms 113–118.
12 Mk. 14:26.
13 *Letters* xcvi, 7.

when to keep in with these same un-Christian Christians he condemned the peasants for their economic uprising in the "Peasants' War" and blasted the hopes which he had earlier raised in their breasts, song died; formality and perfunctoriness crept into the Reformed services; choirs took the place of popular singing; the organ expanded its function until it dominated the service, not only embroidering the grand chorales with jigsaw patterns of accompaniment and separating the stanzas with long-drawn-out frilly interludes, but literally covering up the rags of a poverty-stricken Christianity with a gorgeous cloak of thunder.[14]

This flood tide and recession is clearly marked in England also. During the persecutions of Bloody Mary, thousands of Puritans fled to Germany and Geneva. There they became infected with the enthusiasm of their fighting brothers of the continent. For Calvin had brought to his side Louis Bourgeois, French master of song, and together they trained those people in the art of communal singing, unknown hitherto in their home land. Returning to England, they sang their metrical Psalms with all their might, first in London, then all over England and Scotland, crowds of people, thousands of them, in the streets at all hours of the day and night— to the great disgust of Queen Elizabeth who dubbed their tunes "Geneva jiggs." [15] But when British religion became the shuttle-cock of politics, when Parliament controlled the Church, and Puritan or Whig or Tory Ministries dispensed fat "livings" to subservient favorites, then the light faded, Psalm-singing dwindled to a nasal drawl, enthusiasm died, and the organ buried the corpse. Genuine religious song had again to await a genuine grass-roots resurrection of religion. George Whitefield and the Wesleys were the Gabriels who

---

[14] See Rutland Boughton: *Bach, the Master,* 1930, Chap. 3.
[15] Letter by John Jewell, Bishop of Salisbury, dated Mar. 5, 1660; also Isaac Disraeli: *Curiosities of Literature,* 1882, page 349.

blew the fateful trumpet and aroused once more the lyric spirit of England.

One word should be added about what religious music does to a person.

Music is a direct stimulus to our internal organs which are the chief seat of our emotions. It can arouse almost any emotion from anger and the fighting spirit to worship. What it does to us on a given occasion is determined largely by its concomitants and by the memories and associations it arouses. In church the architecture induces certain trains of thought as well as feeling. You are there reminded of the age-old institution of which you are a part, of the historic and the personal experiences that have here found a home, of the obligations and the privileges of worship, communion, fellowship, consecration. Music that in other contexts might evoke secular dreams or relaxations or loves, in that ecclesiastical setting elevates the soul to spiritual altitudes. Perhaps memory with its surcharges of emotion plays the most important part—recollections of the early religious awakening of one's youth, of baptisms, confirmations, of companions long since scattered, of parents who once worshipped here and are now in heaven, and of high resolves once made and then forgotten, of bright visions now lost awhile. Music opens up the soul, and what is within comes streaming to the surface on the tide of harmony.

But these emotions need not be confined to an ecclesiastical environment. A voice can perform the miracle anywhere. The character and sincerity of the singer may be the evocative force—as when Marian Anderson sang the negro spiritual, "And he never said a mumblin' word" to an audience in Salzburg. Says Vincent Sheehan: [16]

Hardly anybody in the audience understood English well enough to follow what she was saying, and yet the immense sor-

---

[16] *Between the Thunder and the Sun*, Random House, 1943, page 25.

row—something more than the sorrow of a single person—that weighted her tones and lay over her dusky, angular face, was enough. At the end of this spiritual there was no applause at all —a silence instinctive, natural and intense, so that you were afraid to breathe. She frightened us with the conception of a mighty suffering.

I myself remember something similar: a large audience of Negroes in Indianapolis at the request of the preacher, Dr. E. Stanley Jones, sang, "Were you there when they crucified my Lord?" The emotion aroused was intense, as if one were witnessing the age-old frustration of a gifted race.

I remember the Gregorian singing of the monks of Quarr Abbey, Isle of Wight. The men flitted in silently like black moths and, standing in their stalls, they sang the service to the barely audible accompaniment of the organ. The plain-song rose and fell in one united voice, soft, introspective; it flowed like an eddying stream through the intricate melismas; it was selfless, upward-looking, like the face of Christ in Raphael's *Transfiguration*. This was not music only; it was worship.

I remember the Litany in St. Paul's, London. The organ like a tide bore along alternately the feeble voice of the priest as he recalled the dangers and the sins from which we sought deliverance, and the angelic tones of the boy choristers mingled with the muffled roar of the great congregation as they besought heaven's grace—

Good Lord, deliver us. Good Lord, deliver us—

until like storm waves breaking upon the shore, the quick-recurring petition beat importunately against the gates of heaven:

We beseech Thee to hear us, Good Lord.
We beseech Thee to hear us, Good Lord.

That was penitence and pleading.

I remember St. Joan of Arc's Day in Notre Dame, Paris. The great cathedral was thronged with 15,000 people. I could not see the altar from where I stood in the triforium, but I could hear the organ—majestic, triumphant; and I could feel the earth-shaking trumpet-bass stir to action every fiber of my being. That was the Church Militant.

I remember the Sunday afternoons at home in the big living-room when the children gathered about us for the hymn hour. There were the oldest daughter—or her sister—at the piano, the youngest son with his clarinet, a middle child with her violin, another couple with mandolins, and still another at the organ. And one was not, for God had taken him from his fighting plane in the sky—but we could hear him singing. And we all sang the old simple words and the favorite music while their mother and I sat hand in hand on the well-worn sofa. Someone has said, "When Bach plays, God goes to the Mass." Well, He came down every Sunday to our house—until time scattered the musicians to the ends of the earth. That was a large segment of religion—joy, companionship, loyalty, trust, love, worship—and music was its vehicle.

In his vivid and picturesque way Professor Smith has approached this subject from the point of view of the liturgist and choral director. His wide experience in this field enables him to offer practical suggestions for the enrichment of our religious services; and his survey of the development of church music will suggest to choir masters how they may approach their problems of interpretation historically. This is essential equipment.

## IV

We are indebted to the late President Beaven of the Colgate-Rochester Divinity School for the suggestion—one might almost say the mandate—that Dr. Eastman adopt the unique point of view presented in the last lecture of this series. Instead of emphasizing the fact that in the past drama has been, or in the present is or may be, an authentic expression of religion, Dr. Eastman has shown how dramatic presentation is by its very essence the technique par excellence for the propagation of religion. Accordingly what on the surface appears to be a technical discussion that has value chiefly for preachers, when considered more deeply proves to be an insight into the essential nature of one of the greatest of the arts. No one, even if he be a layman, can read what is there presented without feeling enriched and uplifted. He will think of this chapter hereafter whenever he goes to church; and when he attends a serious play he will find himself realizing that the problems there revealed and the tensions developed have their real solution and release only in religion.

In its origin and earliest development drama had to do with religion. The annual mystery play at Abydos in Egypt, 4000 years and more ago, enacted dramatically the death and resurrection of Osiris. Both actors and spectators re-fought the ancient battle, buried the statue of the god and on the third day exumed it. In its modern parallel in the Greek Orthodox ritual the faithful likewise carry a crucifix in procession through the city, bury it beneath the high altar on Good Friday and recover it on Easter morning. The miracle plays of the middle ages were the Church's favorite technique of making vivid the essentials of the Christian faith. But in the case of the drama, as of the three other arts discussed in this series, the method of presentation was too good to be preëmpted by a single interest. As Luther once said that it was too bad for the devil to have all the best tunes, so the world insisted that the Church should not monopolize the most powerful medium of instruction known; with the result that the world took over the drama and in the Restoration days of England completely debauched it. This led to the total abandonment of drama by the Church. John Wesley had abundant reason for prohibiting the theater to his Methodists.

It remained therefore for the "world" to revive the drama as a social and moral force, even as it had been in Greek times. This revival took place in the late nineteenth century, paralleling the resurgence of the Social Gospel and of those humanitarian forces in England released by organizations like the Fabian Society, of which the dramatist, George Bernard Shaw, was a founder. The break with the tawdry and often insipid plays of the Victorian age is generally credited, however, to the Norwegian Ibsen—and that break was destined to have tremendous significance. Ibsen concentrated upon folks rather than upon artificial plots; he began to look upon the insides of persons, their relations to one another and to the social situation in which their lives were set. His *Enemy of the People* was powerful social criticism; *The Doll's House,* besides being an important psychological study, was a biting attack against the then current concept of women as pretty ornaments. In England, Shaw and Galsworthy took up the cudgels for social righteousness in plays like *Androcles* and *Loyalties.* Shaw's *Saint Joan* is one of the greatest religious dramas of all time. Something of the animus behind it, his disgust with modern materialism and its pseudo-scientific approach to morals and religion, he has voiced in the Preface to the play from which, owing to the restrictions Shaw has placed upon his publisher, I am not privileged to quote. I recommend the Preface to your attention as a piece of Shavian prose at its best.

The social drama of the past fifty years has been essentially religious because it has been essentially ethical. The Church's "prodigal son" has returned—but not yet to the Church; it has come as an instrument of social analysis and criticism, sometimes even of religious insight.

*Tobacco Road* could not have achieved its record run on

the basis of its scandalous language alone; it reveals beneath its sordid surface a social cancer that cries for the surgeon's knife. Any of the plays broadcast in 1940–41 by the Free Company [17] will make an American citizen realize that liberty under law is a possession dearer than life itself, one that confers upon the individual a dignity and worth comparable to the best gifts of religion. In a more strictly religious field, Marc Connelly's *Green Pastures* presents an insight into the heart of God seldom attained in church; and Thornton Wilder's *Our Town* brings the perspectives of Eternity into the contemporary scene.

In his oral presentation Dr. Eastman gave two illustrations not retained in his final form. One showed how the endeavor to understand life in dramatic terms gave a person an insight into the greatness of unrecognized people; the other showed how drama based upon a contemporary social problem gripped even the participants in the struggle and moved them in the direction of a religious solution. I have asked Dr. Eastman to reproduce them here:

## TWO ILLUSTRATIONS

THESE STORIES ARE TAKEN from our experience at the Chicago Theological Seminary. The first concerns a young man, a candidate for the ministry, who came into one of my drama classes. His previous training had been largely concentrated in the field of theology. He had been conditioned to think and speak in scientific and theological lingo. He now wanted to write a play, but couldn't get started. His imagination had not yet been thawed out so that he could think and write in terms of characters and conflicts and choices and plot and climax. One of the first assignments I gave him was to discover some central character around whom the action of his

---

[17] *The Free Company Presents,* Dodd, Mead, 1941.

play would revolve. He couldn't think of any such character. The weeks passed and he was still stalled.

He came into my office and asked for some suggestion. I suggested that he think of some character about whom he had read or preferably whom he had known—a character who had wanted something not only for himself but for his fellow men and who had striven for it against great opposition. He said he didn't know of such a character.

"Where did you come from?" I asked.

"From Kansas," he replied.

"Do you mean to tell me that there are no people of that sort in Kansas whom you have known?" He knew of none.

"Well," I said, "I think that is a libel on the state of Kansas. You go back and think further. I will give you another week. If by that time you can't get started on this play, perhaps you had better drop out of the course and take something easier."

Four or five days later he came back, his face aglow.

"I've got him!" he announced.

"Who is it?" I asked.

"It's my old man," he answered. "I never had thought about him in that light; I always thought he was kind of queer. But he started one of the first farmer coöperatives in the state of Kansas. He went through a lot of persecution, and we children suffered some of it. I know that he mortgaged our house in order to pay the deficit of that coöperative the first year. He met a lot of opposition from the local merchants and others who thought that coöperatives were works of the devil. But today the coöperative is going strong."

"Very well," I said. "Go ahead and write your play around him." He plunged into the task with enthusiasm. Just before Christmas he returned with the play completed. He brought it to me all beautifully bound and tied up with blue and pink ribbons—a sort of baby's layette for his brain child.

"What are you going to do with it?" I asked.

"I am going to give it to my father for his Christmas present," he answered.

I think his father probably never received a Christmas present he appreciated more. This play had opened the boy's own eyes to appreciation and understanding. His father was no longer queer, but the hero of his play. If an art course does nothing further than that for a student, perhaps it justifies itself.

The other story illustrates the use of drama as a reconciling force in the midst of a social conflict. Several years ago we had such a conflict in the form of a milk strike. The farmers who produced the milk for Chicago claimed that they were not receiving the cost of production. The milk distributors refused to pay more. Consumers clamored for cheap milk and the City Health Department insisted on pure milk. Emotional tensions reached the breaking point. Violence followed. Blood was shed. Hundreds of thousands of gallons of milk were dumped into ditches.

Into that situation the late Professor Arthur Holt turned his research students in Social Ethics. He sent them out into the homes of the farmers—into the offices of the milk drivers' union—and into every other spot where they were allowed to enter. He wanted *the facts*. One day he came into my office with a large bundle of manuscripts. "Here," he said, "are the reports—the case studies—my students have been making of this situation. The stuff is loaded with emotional dynamite. It's dramatic. Do you suppose your students could dramatize it?" We talked it over. The students dramatized it—trying not to write propaganda for one side or the other, but to show all sides fairly and to shed some light of religion on the whole dark scene.

Then one night we produced it in Graham Taylor Hall. Dr. Holt invited a picked audience to that first production, an audience made of the striking farmers, the milk drivers' union, and the city health department. Mind you, these men had been engaged for weeks in a bitter contest. The curtain went up. For half an hour the only sounds in that crowded room were those of the players. Then the curtain closed. A farmer got to his feet. "Mr. Chairman," he said, "I move you that we have this play presented in every church and school house in this area." A milk-drivers' union man seconded the motion. It carried without a dissenting vote.

About two weeks later Dr. Holt came into my office again.

"I've just come from a meeting where the milk strike was settled," he said. "I'm not sure how much our play had to do with it, but I thought you would be interested to know that during an intermission we got to talking about it, and we found that 16 of the 24 men who sat in at the peace conference had been here that night to see the play."

# I

# THE EXPRESSION OF RELIGION IN PAINTING AND SCULPTURE

*By* ALBERT EDWARD BAILEY

PROFESSOR ALBERT EDWARD BAILEY, M.A. has given a life-time to studying religion in art. For many years he has been actively engaged in teaching the subject of Religious Art. His first professorial appointment was to the Faculty of Boston University, where he remained for ten years. Later he occupied the chair of Religion and Art in the Central Y.M.C.A. College in Chicago, and has been guest professor at various colleges and theological seminaries. Coincident with his teaching he frequently appeared as a popular lecturer on the Bible and Art. Material for his teaching and lecturing was gathered by many trips to Europe, Palestine and Bible Lands, and two trips to the Orient.

As an author he is also well and favorably known. Among his published works are "The Gospel in Art" (1916), "The Use of Art in Religious Education" (1921), "Christ in Recent Art" (1935), "Art and Character" (1938), "Jesus and His Teachings: the Approach Through Art" (1942), "Daily Life in Bible Times" (1943). His interpretations of religious pictures in *The Upper Room* regularly reach an audience of 1,700,000 in four languages and Braille.

# I

## THE EXPRESSION OF RELIGION IN PAINTING AND SCULPTURE

IN THE SHORT SPACE allowed for the consideration of so huge a subject, I have thought it best to be objective rather than philosophical; to show you what ends religious art has served and to refer to specific works that illustrate them. These ends may be stated briefly as follows:

(1) The symbolic presentation of divine beings
(2) The factual representation of human beings associated with the history of religion
(3) The presentation of the dogmas of faith; propaganda
(4) What the Hindus call "bhakti"—the symbolic offering of one's self or one's work to God
(5) Social amelioration

In the interest of vividness I shall ask you to construct in your imagination a Museum of Religious Art, arranged along the lines just suggested. Here it is—a substantial structure of five rooms, most of them subdivided into alcoves for further classification. We shall walk through this museum together while I, as docent, will try to point out the significance of what we see. Shall we enter?

### ROOM I

The first room is devoted to the pictorial presentation of divinity. Over the door I have placed two Egyptian hieroglyphics that mean "the beautiful gods." The character for "gods" is an upright ax followed by the plural sign; that for "beautiful" is a lute. We discover at once that hieroglyphics are a most ancient art product and that they are saturated with symbolism. The ax is the symbol of power and authority —as it was in the sign of the late Fascist party in Italy; the lute is made to produce melody and harmony. One might therefore define the Egyptian conception of divinities as those spiritual powers which may be used for the enhancement of life. At this point we might adopt as a tentative definition of religion, the urge of the soul to make helpful contact with unseen sources of power and joy.

In Alcove A have been placed the most primitive divinities, which are animals and birds. These are characteristic of the religion called Animism in which various objects in nature are regarded as the residence of spirits. These objects were stones or trees, but more often were living creatures whose actions seemed to men to be mysterious and wise. Pictures of them with the aid of medicine men have been used by all primitive people in the struggle for existence.

Here are some of those ancient symbols, drawn or painted on walls and on papyri or carved in relief: From Egypt— Horus the hawk, Kheper the beetle, Amon the ram, Hathor the cow; from India—Ganesha the elephant, Hanuman the monkey, Garuda the eagle; from Alaska—standing in the center of the alcove—a totem pole, which is the Indian's confession of faith: "I believe in the Old Raven, maker of heaven and earth, and in the Young Raven his son, begetter of men; and in Hy-yi-shon-a-gu the bear, who holds up the earth."

We must not inquire where the Raven or the Crocodile or the Elephant or the pictures of them leave off and the divine spirit in them begins; they all interpenetrate and are all, partly at least, subject to control.

In Alcove B we perceive that the artist has followed man upward in enlarging his concepts of divine powers. The Nature gods have arrived: first the Sun, source of all life, the dying and rising vegetation on which man's continued existence depends, the heavens with their blue and their stars. To be sure, the old animals persist, but they now are subservient, are emblems of the cosmic powers. The hawk and the scarab become an artist's shorthand for various functions of the sun (Plate V A). Or, to convey the new idea of the gods as persons and still not to lose touch with the old, the artist paints them with the head of an animal and the body of a man. Anthropomorphic gods are emerging.

Alcove C shows us still more complex conceptions of divinity: sculptured Assyrian cherubs guarding the entrance, symbols of divine protection which were the ancestors of the Israelite Cherubim that guarded the Ark in the Holy of Holies at Jerusalem. A strange composite they are, with the body of a bull to show strength and reproductive power, the wings of an eagle for swiftness of attack or rescue, the bearded head of a man for intelligence, crowned by horns which are the conventional symbol for divinity.

Within the alcove on the left wall hangs a painting in silk, beautiful in line, in composition and color, by the Chinese artist Cho-Shi-Kio, of the Sung Dynasty (A.D. 960–1126).[1] It is called the "Peacock King of Light." The god, with an elaborate crown and a halo of fire, sits upon an open lotus which in turn rests upon the back of a gorgeous peacock. The bird's spread tail fills with its eyes nearly the whole background, while the rest of the space is swirling cloud. Four of the god's six hands hold attributes of his powers and functions while the other two are placed palms together before his breast in an attitude of contemplation. Such a picture performs the functions of visualizing, interpreting and emotionalizing a Buddhist concept of divinity.

The same function is performed for the Hindus by the

---

[1] Imperial Museum, Kyoto, Japan.

"Dance of Shiva," a magnificent copper statue in the center of the alcove (Plate V B). This strange figure represents a cosmic philosophy too abstruse for the common man but in this form made visible and somewhat understandable. The god Shiva has three eyes and four arms, by which are suggested his all-seeing wisdom and his myriad powers of action. In one right hand he holds a drum, at the sound of which the mass of fiery stardust about him takes form as suns and worlds. His second right hand expresses protection and is called the "hand of hope." His upper left hand holds the flame that, after the cycle of creation is complete, destroys life in order that it may be recreated in other cycles of existence. Beneath Shiva's feet is a malignant demon which sought to destroy him; about Shiva's neck is a serpent sent for the same purpose but reduced to impotence by the god's divine power. The long netlike lines behind Shiva's head are his hair whirling in the dance, symbol of the never-ceasing movement and energy at the center of the universe.

The remaining walls of this alcove are covered with replicas of Egyptian tomb and temple decorations and vignettes from papyri. All kinds of gods are depicted in all kinds of situations. Some are seated on thrones to represent their lofty state; they are crowned with elaborate combinations of horns, feathers, cobras, solar discs, each detail meant to recall to the worshipper either a divine attribute or a portion of ritual or an episode in popular mythology. In these pictures the artist has standardized the more important of the innumerable gods and their often contradictory functions; that is to say, he has furnished the imagery by which the chaos of Egyptian religion may be reduced to some sort of order and made comprehensible. We must not underestimate this function. These animals and hybrids may seem to us mere historic relics that have only a curious interest. But we must remember that in their day they were throbbing with life,

PLATE V (A)

SOLAR EMBLEMS

The disc, a scarab, a ram-headed deity. Tomb of Ramses III,
Valley of the Kings, Egypt (twelfth century B.C.)

PLATE V (B)

SIVA DANCING

From South India (fifteenth century). Courtesy of
Trustees of Boston Museum of Fine Arts.

## PLATE VI (A)

ATHENA ASSISTING HERAKLES

Metope of the Zeus Temple, Olympia, Greece
(fifth century B.C.)

## PLATE VI (B)

GOD CREATING ADAM

By Michelangelo, Sistine Chapel, Rome (1512 A.D.)

with power and emotion, and that men went into their presence with awe.

As we proceed to Alcove D, symbolic of man's passing to a higher civilization, we leave behind the animals and the hybrids; for with the advent of the Greek race man became the measure of all things and the state gods became wholly human. With the Greeks art was a practical business. Its chief functions were to assist in the cult of the local heroes and gods, and to help the worshippers visualize superhuman beings more and more adequately. But the Greek artists discovered in the gods not only perfection of physical form; they discovered character. This discovery did not come to them ready-made; it arose from the development of the Greek race through social experience. This shows a progressive affirmation of moral values which parallels the deepening moral insights and then the degeneration of the race. In this alcove, therefore, we have arranged a life history of the goddess Athena. It must be in sculpture because Greek painting has almost entirely perished except in the field of ceramics.

Beginning on the left is a sixth century B.C. statuette of Athena. She is stocky and masculine—a true "Pallas" or brandisher; for, clad in full panoply, she strides into battle, her spear poised to strike down her foes. She is the very personification of the fighting spirit of the primitive Achaeans and Danaans and their Greek successors who conquered the whole east-Mediterranean area.

Next to her is the Athena of the temple of Aegina, early fifth century. Here she is not fighting but directing. She fights with her mind, devises the strategy which lies back of the battle formation; she inspires the courage of her Greeks. Ares may still delight in slaughter, but Athena has emerged as intelligence in war.

Beyond, in the metopes of the Zeus temple at Olympia, early fifth century, the goddess becomes the friend of the hero Herakles (Plate VI A). This Herakles of folk-lore was not a warrior at all but one who toiled for the amelioration of human life; his labors called not only for endurance but social purpose. So here the goddess stands without armor, with a gentle and feminine charm, scheming with her hero to outwit Atlas, and lending a helping hand as he shifts the sky from his shoulder back to that of the giant.

Next to this exhibit stands the beautiful stela from Athens known as the *Mourning Athena*. Her association with man in his hopes and defeats has made the goddess tender. She leans upon her spear and drops a tear on the grave of one of her fallen comrades. Her face is full of gentle sympathy. Here is a goddess who has been "touched with a feeling of our infirmities," as none of the earlier gods of humanity has been.

Last in this ascending series comes the masterpiece of Phideas, the *Athena Parthenos*. Athena is still a warrior, for only yesterday she helped her people beat back the might of Persia; but now she rests after battle—she pushes back her helmet, lays down her shield near the old snake god Erichthonius who was worshipped on this spot before Athena had banished superstition from the minds of men, and in her right hand she holds a figure of Victory. In her minor adornments Phideas has hinted other aspects of her character and deeds. On the shield's edge, the battle of the Amazons against the Titans—symbol of the victory of intelligence over brute force; on her helmet, the winged horses and the sphinx, reminders of her early conquests over nature for man's sake, her instruction in husbandry and the domestication of animals; on her breast the Gorgon's head with snaky locks, symbol of that unapproachable chastity that turns to stone all who would come near to violate it. She was the "Parthenos," the Virgin; and never in the long years of myth-making had any man dared breathe a syllable of slander against her character. And when the awe-struck worshipper raised his eyes to her face he saw features that were lofty, kindly and wise, all that one would expect to find in a daughter of Zeus —a "Logos," who brought down to man's level of comprehension the wisdom of the ineffable godhead.

We have now reached the peak of Greek religious insight. Beyond Phideas stand Praxiteles, the Rhodians, the Graeco-Roman sculptors, who mirror in their gods and goddesses the havoc wrought to faith by the sophists and materialistic philosophers. In the hands of Praxiteles, Hermes becomes a superb play-boy whose least thought is for man's welfare, and Aphrodite becomes a nude courtesan.[2] Under Hellenistic manipulation the gods become gigantic figures in a story, and Athena a psychopathic case.[3]

This case history supports our thesis that art holds a mirror up to the contemporary mind of man. In all these alcoves the symbols that stand for the gods are socially derived; in each metaphor that is used we realize the interplay of the individual who conceives and of the racial culture that conditions the form. Were it not so, the patterns in which the artist expressed himself would have been unintelligible to his contemporaries. The Egyptian symbols and images were to the Greeks, foolishness; Chinese categories of form would have been a stumbling-block to the matter-of-fact seventeenth-century Dutch. Each artist must speak in his own tongue, yet must realize that his language is a social product.

In the fifth and last alcove reserved for pictures of the Christian God these principles still hold. While the general ideas embodied derive from the Greeks, Christian imagery is molded into the contemporary forms of social organization. For example, with the rise of the Byzantine empire and later the Holy Roman empire, God becomes assimilated to the Imperial pattern. Christ, whose idealized face is henceforth

---

[2] Vatican: Cnidian Aphrodite.
[3] British Museum, head, 3rd cent., B.C.

the standard model for the First Person of the Trinity, assumed the dignity of a Justinian; became the "Pantocrator" or All-powerful, and as such looked down in gorgeous mosaics from the domes or apses of Saint Sophia and other Byzantine churches. But the perfect medieval God is that of Van Eyck in the Ghent polyptych, which is our second exhibit in this alcove. Here he is clothed with all the regal magnificence of both the Emperor and the Pope—for it is from Him that authority proceeds downward through both sacred and secular deputies. His symbol of power is not the ax of the Egyptians, nor the thunderbolt of Zeus, but a crystal scepter adorned with gold and precious stones; his symbols of royalty are bejeweled robes and two crowns: the crown of secular rule which lies at his feet, the crown of spiritual rule which is a papal tiara blazing with light upon his head. The relative position of the two crowns shows that in all affairs the Papacy takes precedence over the Empire. This imagery for God dominated the medieval world and lasted at least through the days of Puritan John Milton.

The other picture in this alcove contains the final word of art on the subject of an anthropomorphic God. It is Michelangelo's *Creation of Adam* (Plate VI B). In this artist's thought all regal state would belittle the creator who is above all and in all. Nothing less than pure Personality can be adequate, that form of organization in which creation reaches its climax of intricacy and wonder. And here are the distinguishing traits of this God:

Creative energy, like that which pervades and overflows his body; Intelligence, like that which sharpens his features and animates his eye; Feeling, the sympathetic outreach of his soul that embraces all created things and persons in boundless love.

Here is no limited description—God as King, God as Pope, God as an aloof Olympian, God as sun or star; but

God as the universal and complete Person, whose characteristics may be dimly discerned by our twentieth-century science in the realms of physics and chemistry, of mathematics, biology and psychology. It is no accident that this superb symbol should arise in the days of the Italian Renaissance when man awoke to the wonder and beauty of this world as contrasted with the "other world" of theology and of the schoolmen; when personalities of high potential were emerging in various fields of activity and when art became glorious through the creative genius of men like Michelangelo himself. One might almost say that the artist has here painted the portrait of his own soul, freed from the inner conflicts that made his life a tragedy.

Before we leave this first room of our Museum, we must look back across its five alcoves for a final summary. We have seen the artist at work supplying the imagery with which mankind has been able to think about God. This imagery is a reflection always of the culture from which it has arisen. It records for the eye what myth and tradition and ritual have transmitted through the ear; it documents the growth of ideas from primitive animistic concepts, through subhuman or hybrid to anthropomorphic symbols that reflect the growing social experience of man; and it culminates in man's ultimate insight into God as Personality. Art cannot take us beyond this point. When science arises to penetrate the mysteries behind phenomena it has to abandon the symbols of art for the symbols of mathematics.

## Room II

We now enter the second main gallery of our Museum of Religious Art and there view man's endeavor to visualize the human persons associated with his religion; the authors of the Faiths of mankind, the apostles and martyrs and saints. For centuries the portraits of these men have been spread over the outside of buildings as sculpture, over the inside as fresco or mosaic or stained glass; and as statues or altar pieces they people the chapels and niches of all places of worship. Surely these works must have been created to meet some deep human need.

Our first Alcove, A, is devoted to non-Christian religions. Chief among the founders of these religions is Prince Siddhartha of India. From the stupa gates and rails of Sanchi (Plate VII A) and Gandhara, the temples of Buddh-Gaya and Borobudur and Angkor Wat we have reproduced the thickly crowded reliefs which immortalize the whole story of this man who became the Buddha: his divine conception, his secluded life of pleasure in the royal palace, his discovery of the fact of suffering and death, his search for enlighten-ment among the sages of the forest, his meditation under the bo-tree, his attainment of insight into the nature of suffering and its surcease in Nirvana, his renunciation of blessedness until he could teach the world his secret, his years of mendi-cancy and his final release. These sculptures are both com-memorative and didactic, a conscious endeavor to make vivid the life of the Saviour Buddha and to preach his doctrines of kindness, self-discipline, Karma, and the ultimate extinc-tion of the will to live. Probably no art in the world has had such an influence.

Beyond these Buddhistic reliefs we place illustrations from the Hindu epic, the *Ramayana;* pictures of the Chinese "rakan" or sages in their forests of contemplation; Moham-med's *Ascent to Heaven* by the Persian miniaturist Mirak; and finally the vase paintings of the Greeks. These Greek masterpieces of freehand representation give us illustrations of the legends associated with the shrines of those heroes who mingled with the gods, the cult of whom corresponds some-what to the veneration paid to saints in the Christian pan-theon. On these vases Herakles performs his altruistic labors

PLATE VII (A)

SCULPTURED RAIL, SANCHI, INDIA

Buddhist (fifth—third century, B.C.)

PLATE VII (B)

FRESCOES OF SS. PETER AND PAUL.

Catacomb in Rome (early third century)

PLATE VIII (A)

HERAKLES, AIDED BY ATHENA, CAPTURES CERBERUS, THE HOUND OF HADES

Greek vase painting (sixth century, B.C.)

PLATE VIII (B)

CHRIST RAISES LAZARUS

Karlsruhe Gospels, Romanesque (c. 1150 A.D.)

(Plate VIII A) and feasts with Athena; Perseus, aided by Athena and Hermes, frees Andromeda from her monster; Theseus kills the Minotaur; Orpheus plays his lyre among the Thracians; the Homeric heroes fight around Troy and even contend with the gods. Here religious mythology merges with secular, patriotism and the cultus find common ground, and art performs its old function of creating imagery, immortalizing story, and suffusing all with emotion.

Alcove B contains Christian examples of saints, martyrs and heroes, including Christ who is represented in art as both God and man. In the first two centuries, owing to various repressions, the pictorial expressions of Christianity were few and all of them symbolic. But when the original apostles and their successors died, the visual memories of these venerated ones became dim and needed to be renewed. The earliest renewal came at Rome. First therefore we encounter Saints Peter and Paul, reproduced on our walls from a catacomb in the Viale Manzoni (Plate VII B). Since these frescoes date not later than 217 A.D., without doubt they embody a living tradition. By the third century, Christ begins to be represented rather than symbolized, both in fresco and sculpture. His face has become standardized either as youthful and beardless, as in the Alexandrian tradition, or more mature and bearded as in the Palestine and Syrian style. Stories of his life are now set forth realistically, as in the Dura-Europos fresco of the *Healing of the Paralytic,* one of the earliest on record, early third century.

As Christianity spread to the far corners of the world and new generations of converts arose, the practical need increased of visualizing the persons and events which differentiated this faith from all others. Artists responded everywhere with pictures on chapel walls until even the unlettered could say, "That is our Lord and Saviour; these are the things he did; these are his helpers and missionaries; these are the

Fathers who have explained to the Church the mysteries of our religion." There is room in this alcove to show only a fraction of those innumerable saints whose lives constitute the history of the Church: the frescoes and the altarpieces, and then the statues which crowd the exterior and the interior of cathedrals in all countries and which were intended to be a textbook for the unlearned. In the hands of the sculptors and painters, under the direction of Popes and Bishops, art became consciously the handmaid of religion and was used by the Church as its most effective instrument of spreading the faith.

The most precious objects in Room II are kept under lock and key in Alcove C, the alcove of illustrated Bibles. The earliest surviving specimen is a fifth-century *Septuagint,* probably from Alexandria, with features that hint of second-century ancestors. Next to it is a Vatican parchment with drawings illustrative of the *Book of Joshua,* date about 700 A.D.; and then the gorgeous Paris *Psalter* with full page miniatures in color, in style something like the frescoes of Pompeii. Since there are no Christian allusions in these books they are probably Jewish; and therefore they testify that the human desire for vivid imagery proved ultimately to be stronger than the Second Commandment. These Jewish pictures made a continuous impression upon Christian artists who copied and recopied them through many centuries. Here is the first Christian illustrated Old Testament, the *Cotton Genesis* (British Museum) dating from the sixth century; and next to it the earliest illustrated Gospel—the *Codex Rossano,* made probably in Antioch about the year 500. Its pictures are in the spirit of the oriental story-teller; the motifs are such as appear in the contemporary mosaics from Antioch now to be seen in the museums at Worcester, Baltimore, and Princeton University. Those oft-repeated early patterns reached a climax of splendor in the twelfth century *Octateuch* from Constantinople, with 350 miniatures in blue and gold. The same themes continue not only in the illustrated Gospels of the Romanesque and Gothic periods (Plate VIII B), but in sarcophagi, ivories, mosaics, and even in frescoes of the Italian Renaissance. As late as 1766 a large Armenian textile which we shall borrow for our Museum from the First Baptist Church of Worcester, shows among its 26 pictures a representation of the Ascension which has come down practically unchanged from the *Rabula Gospels,* written in Mesopotamia in 586 A.D. Such a remarkable longevity testifies to the constant human demand for pictorial satisfaction and to the unique service of art to religion.

### Room III

Leaving this room of religious biography and history, we now enter Room III, the treasure-house of Dogma. We are now about to see how art through the centuries has made concrete certain ideas about the spiritual world, the hopes and fears and affirmations by which man lays hold upon life eternal.

Earliest among these beliefs were those connected with life after death, the art expression of which is assembled in Alcove A. The sturdiest believers in that life were the Egyptians. Not only did they believe, but they were willing to invest enormous sums of money to back up their faith, to provide the physical equipment which through magic would accomplish the desired result. We have assembled in this alcove specimens of that equipment—beautiful mummies, coffins, furniture, chests, vases, jewelry; replicas of the sculptures which adorned every foot of the interior of the tomb, portrait statues of the deceased in which his "Ka" could reside; paintings which in humbler tombs, took the place of reliefs or which described in the papyrus *Book of the Dead* all the experiences through which the deceased would pass.

Never in history has art been so necessary to religion and so positive in its affirmations. Through it the dead of a hundred generations speak, and they utter the following credo:

I believe in life after death.

I believe that my body, preserved by the arts of the embalmer, shall again serve as my habitation; and that the portrait statues I place in the tomb will be equally serviceable to my "ka" or double.

I believe that my physical wants will be cared for through the pictures on the walls of my tomb; that by the power of magic impregnated in them by the mortuary priests, the painted servants will plow and sow, irrigate and cultivate, reap and winnow, grind and bake; that cows will calve and give me milk, that game will be driven into my nets, that vines will yield me wine, and that lotus flowers will be eternally sweet.

I believe that the goddess Hathor will meet me on my setting out for the Western Land, and by her divine milk will make me strong; that Osiris, who once was dead but is alive forevermore, and in whose mummied form I am laid to rest, will call me by his own name and admit me to the company of the gods.

But on the other hand I believe that I shall give an account for the deeds done in the body; that my heart will be weighed in the balances in the Judgment-hall of Osiris, and that only after I have met the test of Truth will Horus lead me to his father's throne where I shall hear the Lord of eternity say, "Thou hast been faithful over a few things; enter thou into the joy of thy Lord."

All this the Egyptian believed, and much more; and all of it was pictured with infinite detail, and a copy of the illustrated guidebook called *The Going Forth By Day* was placed in the hand of the deceased so that he might conquer every foe and rise superior to every emergency.

We may well suspect that the priests of the various religions of the world have used men's hopes and fears to frighten them or entice them into the orthodox path; for religious art abounds in flights of pious imagination which picture the delights of heaven and the tortures of hell. The Buddhist monks have equalled the best in the vigor of their imagery. We present a Chinese Heaven presided over by Amitaba-Buddha, painted on silk; and a Buddhist Hell from the Temple of the Tooth in Kandy, Ceylon. One such example is enough!

Christian art has employed similar imagery to the same moral ends. Nearly always the pictures have taken the form of a *Last Judgment*. The Church prescribed the location of this composition; it had to be over the central western entrance of a church, in sculpture if outside, in fresco if inside; for in such a position it could not be overlooked, especially by kings and princes for whom this particular portal was usually reserved. Its joys and terrors were powerful reminders that man's eternal state for weal or woe is fixed by his attitude toward the Church and its sacraments. We show such a one from the portal of Bourges cathedral—a thirteenth-century carved lintel (Plate IX A). In the center an angel holds the scales of Judgment; on his right hand smiling souls follow Peter to the gate of Paradise within which sits Abraham with a bosomful of little souls in the fold of his garment; on the left a riotous crowd of devils, male and female, hurry the lost souls to the eternal bonfire which two imps are super-heating with a pair of bellows.

One entire wall of this alcove is reserved for the *Last Judgment* of Michelangelo, from the Sistine chapel. It is the most terrible one in the world, not because the physical tortures of Hell are depicted, but because the sinners are suffering the pangs of outraged conscience, and saints are trembling as they see the execution of God's righteous law. And the composition is so arranged that when the Popes stand beneath it at the high Altar to celebrate the Mass, they look straight into the jaws of Hell. This is an artist-prophet's denunciation of the papacy, which in his day had reached its lowest depths of paganism.

Alcove B of the Hall of Dogma is filled with symbols of Salvation and the means of attaining it. Every religion has its own imagery. In Buddhism it is the *Wheel of the Law.* This Wheel is one of the most persistent of Buddhist themes, having been devised, it is said, by Gautama Buddha himself, and perpetuated through the centuries by the monk-artists of many countries. The wheel stands for the fixed relationship of cause and effect. At the center are the three root desires which are the dynamic of all life—lust, anger and sloth. Arranged in the divisions made by the spokes of the wheel are symbols of the six states of existence in the universe and the twelve states of feeling and action which succeed one another inexorably in life. Only by suppressing the three root drives can the round of reincarnation be stopped. But outside the wheel, embracing it with all its might, is the Demon of Self, who will cling to it through multitudes of incarnations until he realizes the value of Buddha's way of release, and follows it—the way of renunciation, self-discipline, and kindness.

Whereas the Buddhist found life to be essentially bad and sought escape from it, the early Christians believed that life was good, and could be made better. In those first centuries of our era, when the whole pagan world seemed to be haunted by a sense of sin, and when purification—cleansing and deliverance from sin and death—was the goal of all the Mystery religions, whether the ancient Eleusinian, the Orphic, Dionysiac, Mithraic or those of Isis, the earliest Christian frescoes in the catacombs from the end of the second century through the fourth, breathed confidence that through Christ this purification had been achieved. But true to the psychology of repression, the themes were drawn from the Jewish past: —Noah's Ark of safety as the Church to which the soul may flee; the Rock smitten by Moses as the Church gushing with the Water of Life; the Three Worthies in the Furnace

PLATE IX (A)

THE LAST JUDGEMENT

Sculptured lintel from Bourges Cathedral, France (thirteenth century)

PLATE IX (B)

THREE WORTHIES IN THE FURNACE

Christian sarcophagus, Rome (fourth century)

PLATE X (A)

THE CRUCIFIXION (DETAIL)

By Fra Angelico

S. Marco Monastery, Florence, Italy (1443 A.D.)

PLATE X (B)

PARABLE OF THE TWO HOUSES

A Reformation cartoon, Germany (sixteenth century)

as Christians saved from persecution by the presence of Christ (Plate IX B); Isaac snatched from death by divine interposition, and Jonah rescued from his living tomb. These are all emblems of salvation. It is probable that what determined the choice of these themes by the artist was the use of the same allusions in the prayers of the Early Church. In survivals like the prayers of St. Cyprian of Antioch and the prayer for the dying called *Commendatio Animae,* God is besought to "free the soul as Thou didst free Noah from the Flood, Isaac from the hand of his father Abraham, Daniel from the Den of Lions, the Three Youths from the furnace of burning fuel, etc." In our alcove are replicas not only of the best of these but of certain mosaics and reliefs from sarcophagi; for when Christianity came out from under ground in the fourth century and filled the cemeteries in and around the churches with sculptured coffins, the old themes were repeated. The early mosaics, also, as in the nave of S. Maria Maggiore, Rome, present Old Testament history as a prophecy of the Logos who was destined to redeem the world from sin.

Under this category of Dogmatic Art are found the doctrines which were declared by Church councils to be victorious over heretical ones. Here is a mosaic recently recovered in St. Sophia—an enthroned Virgin adored on either side by Constantine and Justinian. Her doctrinal status is indicated by two large medallions proclaiming her to be "The Mother of God" as decreed by the Council of Chalcedon in 451; while in S. Maria in Domnica, Rome, the enthroned Mary, surrounded by angels, quite usurps the place of Christ in the apse mosaic, and so completes her apotheosis.

The Festivals of the Church, each one a ritualistic reminder of some essential doctrine, are paralleled in art by altarpieces sometimes devoted to a single theme and sometimes portraying all twelve festivals in a single composition. In Byzantine times the emphasis was primarily intellectual; the picture said, "This is what the Church teaches." And because of this didactic purpose the dogma had to be presented with clearness and with no seductive realism that would focus the attention on the form rather than on the substance; and yet the picture managed to convey to the worshipper "the deep emotion that is stirred by the contemplation of mystery." [4]

In this same category of dogmatic painting belong most of the great pictures of the Renaissance period. These pictures came into being not because they were spontaneous expressions of belief on the part of the artist but because they were ordered and paid for by someone who felt that a donation of this kind to some particular church or chapel would enhance his worldly or spiritual prospects. In this spirit, the Duke of Urbino ordered from Justus of Ghent that unusual *Last Supper* for the church of Sant' Agatha in Urbino (1475), which is really the doctrine of *Transubstantiation,* and which contains the duke's own portrait and that of a visiting Persian ambassador. Similarly, the papal exchequer paid Raphael for his fresco in the Vatican called the *Disputa,* which exhibits the doctrine of the *Mass* as one of the Church's most exalted mysteries.

The allied mystery of the *Trinity* has been painted in many symbolic forms, from the geometrical design of intertwined circles to the complex vision of Dürer, Vienna Gal, in which scores of martyrs, saints, angels and ecclesiastics hover in the sky in adoration of the Godhead.

The pictures of the *Incarnation* are legion. The earliest presentation is the Madonna of the catacomb of Priscilla, Rome, early third century, where the prophet Isaiah stands opposite the Virgin and points to a star above her head in token that his prophecy has been fulfilled. A complete statement of the doctrine is given by Van der Goes (1475), in a

---

[4] Prof. Charles R. Morey: *Medieval Art,* 1942.

picture ordered by Tommaso Portinari, a Medici banker, for the hospital of S. Maria Nuova, Florence. There Mary, Joseph, the shepherds and a dozen angels adore a self-conscious divinity in the form of an infant lying in a bed of light on the floor of a palatial stable.

The *Atonement* has also been presented a thousand times, in sculptured crucifixes, in painted frescoes and altarpieces; and until recent times, when the crucifixion is given as a historical scene, the mystery of redemption by the death of the God-Man has been the burden. Most explicit of all such paintings is the *Crucifixion* by Fra Angelico in the chapter-house of San Marco, Florence, made at the behest of Cosimo de' Medici, 1443 (Plate X A). There a silent company of the apostles, saints, martyrs, ascetics, ecclesiastics, representing the holy Church throughout all the world, kneels in adoration before the great Sacrifice, the meaning of which is shown symbolically, first by the pelican in the frame above Christ's head, and second by the skull of Adam in a niche under Calvary, upon which flows the life-giving blood from the wounded victim. "For as in Adam all die, so in Christ shall all be made alive."

These are only a handful from the thousands of scenes from the lives of Mary and of Christ which were painted not with biographical or historical intent but to embody the Church's teachings about man's fall, the promised Messiah, the fulfillment in Christ, the sacraments by which salvation is mediated to a sinful world, the rewards and punishments which await the revelation of judgment.

Akin to didactic art is the art of propaganda, which is presented in Alcove C. This art becomes impassioned, aggressive, even vituperative. It is not generally realized that the Reformation in Germany was consummated in no small degree by the shock troops of the engravers who flooded the market with prints which presented not so much the truths maintained by the Catholic and Protestant protagonists but the half-truths, the party slogans, distortions, and personal slanders of the leaders. They drove home their points by means of satire and caricature. Because these prints could be produced cheaply and in quantity, and sold not only in bookshops but at market-places and fairs, the public, aroused by the violent religious discussions of the time, was greedy for them. Of the many examples which are shown here I shall describe only one. It is a woodcut entitled the *Parable of the Two Houses*:[5] (Plate X B).

The "House on the Solid Rock" is shown resting on the pillars of the Old Testament, the New Testament, and the Lamb of God, which in turn are based on the solid platform of Christ.

The "House on the Sands" is pillared on the Decretals of the Church, Duns Scotus the Philosopher, and the seven-headed monster Antichrist. The house is splitting in two under the impact of a river labelled, "The Word of God." Above is a scroll inscribed, "Thus is Babylon fallen," and below is a man holding one of Titzel's indulgences.

While most of these prints were made by second-rate artists or worse, some of them are signed by Lucas Cranach, Holbein the Younger, and Dürer. These engravers had great influence in their day not only by their propaganda prints but especially through their homely, naturalistic, and unecclesiastical rendering of Biblical and doctrinal themes emotionalized by their own genuine faith and humanized by their translation into the Germanic idiom. Such works of genuine religion are the *Passion Series* by Dürer, Wohlgemut and Schongauer. In a real sense, all doctrinal art is propaganda, either for home or foreign consumption.

Luther won his battle for a more Biblical religion partly at least with such weapons. In the print shop of Lucas

[5] Matt. 7: 24–27.

Cranach he coöperated actively in the production of illustrated Bibles which culminated in the complete edition of 1534. Thus the Cranach-Luther art Bible takes its place in the long succession which began with the illustrated *Septuagint* of the fifth century and has never ceased.

## Room IV

In the first three galleries we have visited, we have been considering art as a more or less objective phenomenon; art as the visualization of the gods and of persons associated with the cult, as the embodiment of certain doctrines, and as propaganda. Nothing has yet been said about the subjective side of art—art as the expression of the artist's own spiritual life. In Room IV of our Museum we must consider art as "Bhakti"—as the personal offering of the artist to the divinity he worships.

This attitude of the worker is primitive, if not aboriginal, because of the association of art with magic. We can well surmise what must have been the feelings of the Magdalenian artist when, after putting all of his skill into the painting of a mammoth or a bison, by intense concentration he thought out the position of the creature's heart and represented it in its proper place, perhaps while uttering the magic formula that would bring the arrow of the hunter straight to it. We can infer the religious nature of this work from the contemporary practices of pygmies in the Homburi mountains of the Sudan, who after all these thousands of years are practising the magic arts of their ancestors in connection with hunting.[6] And we can understand also the spiritual intensity of the Navajo sandpainter as he lays out on the prepared bed those geometric and symbolic designs which, if faithfully rendered, will bring rain to his people or healing to the sick,

---

[6] L. Frobenius and D. C. Fox: *Prehistoric Rock Pictures in Europe and Africa*, 1937, pp. 22–23.

or express the rituals and the philosophy of his tribe. This is more truly religious art than was the work of many an Italian painter who made altarpieces for his bishop at so much per square foot, with extra pay for gold or lapis lazuli.

The artists of India understood this sacramental aspect of art to a degree unknown in the West; for, from the third century B.C. to the eighteenth A.D., the two dominant springs of artistic production in the East were passionate devotion (*"bhakti"*), to a personal divinity and reunion (*"yoga"*), which is mental concentration carried so far that all distinction between the subject and the object of contemplation is obliterated. This mystic technique used by Hindu and Buddhist artists is as follows:

After ceremonial purification, the artist is to proceed to a solitary place. There he is to perform the "seven-fold office," beginning with the invocation of the hosts of Buddhas and Bodhisattvas, and the offering to them of real or imaginary flowers. Then he must realize in thought the four infinite moods of friendliness, compassion, sympathy, and impartiality. Then he must meditate upon the emptiness or non-existence of all things whereby the five factors of ego-consciousness are destroyed. Then only should he invoke the desired divinity by the utterance of the appropriate "seed-word," and should identify himself completely with the divinity to be represented. Then finally on pronouncing the *dhyana mantram* in which the attributes are defined, the divinity appears visibly, "like a reflection" or "as in a dream," and this brilliant image is the artist's model.[7]

The important thing to note in this process is that the work of art is completed before the work of transcription or representation is begun. What follows is the mechanical embodiment of that realization.

It is difficult to distinguish this description of the creative act of an artist from a description of worship, the object of which likewise is the obliteration of subject and object by

---

[7] Ananda Coomaraswamy: *The Dance of Siva*, 1918, p. 22.

fusion with the god, and the technique of which is in part the practice of visualization. It is not surprising, therefore, to find that the tendency of worshippers in all ages is to identify the pictured divinity with the divinity itself. In other words, worship stimulated by an image becomes iconolatry, or idolatry. Strangely enough, this fact has led the Church at various times to frown upon art. Origen of Alexandria (3rd century) repudiated graven images as fit only for demons.[8] Eusebius of Caesarea (4th cent.) wrote to the sister of the emperor Constantine who had asked for a picture of Christ, that it was "unlawful to possess images pretending to represent the Saviour, either in his divine or his human nature." During this same century, the Synod of Elvira in Spain (306 A.D.) found it necessary to forbid absolutely the painting of pictures of any kind on the walls of churches, in order to guard against the representation of the object of worship.

But the climax of opposition was reached in the Iconoclastic era which lasted 116 years, from 726 to 842 A.D. This feeling against the use of art in religion seems to have stemmed from the East, and behind it lay the age-old Jewish prohibition of images, followed by the Islamic; while the monophysite theology that dominated those regions insisted on the completely supernatural nature of Christ, and so felt that to make Christ human was to degrade him. This controversy was more than academic. During the long struggle, fights were staged in the streets, the churches and monasteries; icon-painters were tortured and iconodule leaders were branded and exiled. So fierce was the destruction that no monument of architecture, sculpture or painting from this period has survived in Istanbul.

This prejudice against representation was quite in keeping

---

[8] *Against Celsus*, Book 3.

with the spirit of Byzantine art, which is mystic and contemplative, and only partly representational. The Western Church, on the other hand, and the Greek-thinking elements everywhere found realistic pictures and statues very helpful.

The Iconoclastic protest against the tendency to worship that which is represented was perhaps intensified by the growth of bibliolatry in the eighth and succeeding centuries; that is, the worship of holy books, such as we have viewed in Room II. Ignorant people who could not read but could understand pictures, treated the illuminated Gospels and Psalters as objects of devotion; and this in turn spurred the illuminator to make his work worthy of the honor which was to be bestowed upon it. Indeed, the defenders of the icons affirmed repeatedly that the Scriptures and the pictures that illustrated them were "equally authoritative as expressions of divine truth; they both gave co-ordinate and equally valid accounts of sacred history." [9] Thus book-making and illuminating became on the part of the monkish artist a work of "bhakti," and on the part of the users a means of mystic union with the divine. This is corroborated by the many colophons in which the writer or illuminator stated that his work was an offering to God for the salvation of his soul; and by the pious records of pilgrims in the holy books they had travelled far to see, praying that their souls might profit as their eyes had rejoiced in the perusal of them. The scriptoria of monasteries were as much places of worship as the chapels where the books were used. Both creation and use were acts of "bhakti."

The last great painter to conceive of his work as a personal offering to God was Fra Angelico (Plate XI A). Among the Italians who by this time were being swept along in the flood-tide of humanism, he almost alone clung to the thirteenth-century ideal of artistic creation as worship. Even a

---

[9] H. R. Willoughby: *The Karahissar Gospels,* Vol. II, p. 76.

PLATE XI (A)

FRA ANGELICO PAINTING

By Merson (nineteenth
century)

PLATE XI (B)

THE DORMITION OF THE
VIRGIN

Window in Chartres
Cathedral, France
(thirteenth century)

PLATE XII

WHITE EAGLE AND PINE TREE

Chinese painting

cursory glance at his work will make us realize the genuineness of his religious feeling.

The most conspicuous modern to practice "bhakti" is William Blake. Blake was wholly absorbed by religion. From his childhood he saw things invisible, walked with God and the saints of the Bible, and in the conscious practice of his art he sought for symbols that would compress into finite shapes the infinite realities with which his soul was in constant communion. Even when he illustrated the Book of Job his real purpose was to use the suffering hero as an allegory of the human soul; the pictures are a chart of the spiritual life of man, a "map of the mystic Way." He identified Christianity with the love and practice of the Fine Arts. "Prayer," said he, "is the study of art; Praise is the practice of art." It has taken the world more than a hundred years to discover the depth of this neglected mystic's spiritual philosophy.

This tradition of religious devotion, expressed through art, has been carried on by such moderns as Holman Hunt, James Tissot, Edouard von Gebhardt, Fritz von Uhde, and many other more obscure workers. In contemporary art the equivalent of "bhakti" appears as the passion for social betterment.

It is permissible to regard the decoration of cathedrals also as primarily a work of "bhakti." Just as the building of the church itself was an offering to God of the money of the wealthy and the work of the artisan and laborer, so the artists who carved the sculpture or designed and made the windows were just as consciously saving their souls; all the more so when, as in Chartres, their work was done not to please an abstract God or a theological Christ, but the most real and ever-present person in the whole realm of their experience —the Virgin Mary (Plate XI B). Listen to the classic paragraph from Henry Adams: [10]

---

[10] *Mont St. Michel and Chartres,* Houghton Mifflin, pp. 161–162.

The glass-worker was in the Virgin's employ; he was decorating her own chamber in her own palace; he wanted to please her. To him, a dream would have been in order. His pay . . . was the same as that of the peasants who were hauling the stone from the quarry at Berchières while he was firing his oven. His reward was to come when he should be promoted to decorate the Queen of Heaven's palace in the New Jerusalem. All this is written in full in every stone and window. The artists were doing their best, not to please a swarm of flat-eared peasants or slow-witted barons, but to satisfy Mary, the Queen of Heaven, to whom the kings and queens of France were coming constantly for help, and whose absolute power was almost the only restraint recognized by emperor, pope and clown.

But if the artist executed the windows of Chartres as an offering to the Virgin, so did the guilds show their devotion by paying for them. They too wanted to serve the Queen of Heaven; and to make sure that she did not overlook that fact they caused their windows to be signed: the merchant tailors, by panels picturing a tailor's shop and a shop-boy showing cloth to a customer. The carpenters and coopers left their signatures likewise, the drapers, the butchers, and the rest. Every thirteenth-century work of art was an offering to God or the Virgin or the saint in whose honor the church was reared.

All votive or commemorative paintings are related to "bhakti." Among the humbler varieties are the *retablos,* so abundant in Mexico—small *ex-votos* painted in oil on a piece of tin. The *ex-voto* masterpieces of the world's museums have been collected from impoverished or abandoned churches where once they occupied places of honor. Wherever the donor is painted alone or with his family as part of the holy group, we may be sure that the spirit of devotion lay behind the gift. A chief place in our Museum is given to the altarpiece in the Church of St. Bavon in Ghent, commonly called *The Adoration of the Lamb,* painted by the Van Eyck brothers in 1432. (Now temporarily in the chateau of Goering!) When the wings of this gorgeous polyptych are closed, on two of its chief outer panels you can see kneeling in adoration the donor, Judocus Vydt, and his wife, Elizabeth Borluut. This gift is their act of participation in the Christian faith, the chief tenets of which are the subject of the twenty-four panels which make up the whole.

In still another alcove of this room of "bhakti" art, we must place certain landscapes, the emotional quality of which betrays the artist's contact with the Infinite whom he has met under the guise of beauty or majesty. To find appropriate examples we shall first revert to the followers of Lao-Tzu, (Chinese, 6th century B.C.) whose philosophy is based upon the idea of the oneness of man with nature, or Tao, and whose discipline was a quiet resting of the soul that Tao might speak to it and through it. For it is from Lao-Tzu, so Laurence Binyon tells us, that "has flowed all that is most glowing and alive in Chinese painting and literature."

Says Lao-Tzu:

> Tao is the source of everything and is present in everything. . . . Your soul in her innermost is Tao. . . . The trees, the mountains, the sea, they are your brothers, like the air and the light. By strifelessness . . . we yield to the inner motive-force which we derive from Tao and which leads us to Tao.[11]

When the Zen sect of Buddhism became dominant in China during the Sung Dynasty (960–1280 A.D.)—a sect that practiced the Taoist doctrine of contemplation—the most characteristic paintings became landscapes or nature subjects (Plate XII). The artists of Persia also, who followed the Sufi theology of Islam, regarded Beauty as the signal of the Holy Presence. Nor is it strange that in the nineteenth to twentieth century, when nature poetry took on the mystic tinge of

---

[11] Henri Borel: *The Rhythm of Life*. Dutton, 1921.

religion; when Wordsworth could write "Tintern Abbey"; Blake, "Little Lamb, Who Made Thee?"; Tennyson, "Flower in the Crannied Wall"; and Sidney Lanier, "The Marshes of Glynn"—to mention only a few—painters should have discovered and expressed the presence of a living soul in the universe or at least should have taken refuge in nature from the world of man which so largely had preoccupied him. Each of you no doubt has a favorite landscapist who has opened for you the mysteries of space and energy, of form and color, which are the garments of the Eternal.

Here is an intimate detail from an artist's life which bears witness to the hunger for the Infinite that will not wholly be denied:

F. Molina-Campos, a contemporary Argentine painter, now doing work in Hollywood, made and sustained a great reputation for twenty years by painting the life of the "gauchos" or cowboys of the vast pampas of his country. The pictures were dramatic, colorful, photographic in their realism except that some caricature was introduced to universalize the types and to prevent sensitive neighbors from feeling hurt. He himself was a gaucho and lived on a ranch; that was the life he knew to the last detail. Suddenly he began to paint landscapes—only a few—the great spaces, the clouds and driving rain, the blue night, all of them transcriptions of emotion; and while he sold his gaucho pictures freely and for big prices, he would never sell a landscape. Finally the landscape he loved best he gave to the friend he loved best. Although the artist was unconscious of it, such paintings reveal an authentic religious experience.

### Room V

The last room in our museum, Room V, is devoted to a type of art which some might not call religious at all. Nevertheless this type, which is quite modern, even contemporary, is a phenomenon parallel to the development within the Church of the Social Gospel, and still later to the tensions and maladjustments which arose during and after World War I. The artists involved might resent the charge of being in any conscious way social gospellers, yet they express in their art the conviction that something is wrong with the social order. Art in general for the last forty years has been reflecting the disintegration of the world. It has been losing its soul. It has expressed in the language of feeling what the philosophers have dignified into a system; that man is a "dust wreath in the cosmic ether," that conduct is a response to stimuli, that ethics is a reaction pattern, and that art has no function but to send esthetic thrills along the *medulla oblongata* of the intelligentsia. The succession of *isms* which followed Cezanne—cubism, futurism, surrealism, and the apotheosis of futility in dadaism—were convincing symptoms that the Decline of the West was on the way.

But now and then certain artist-prophets have emerged from the welter of degeneracy. They either hold up to scorn our sins of greed and the will to power which stare at us from our economic dislocations and the Second World War; or they assert that the values which give life significance are not dead but await our re-affirmation. These men are our counterparts of the prophet Amos:

> For three transgressions of Israel, yea, for four,
> I will not turn away the punishment thereof;
> Because they sold the righteous for silver
> And the poor for a pair of shoes.
> . . . . . . . . . . . . . .
> But let justice roll down like the waters,
> And righteousness as a perennial stream.

In this final room we shall present a synopsis of this prophetic art, the art of social conviction and protest. In the first alcove devoted to War we show a selection from Goya's etchings of the barbarities of the Napoleonic invasion of Spain, a prophet born before his time. Then after nearly a century, the Russian Verestchagin (1874) with his *Apotheosis of War*—a pyramid of skulls "dedicated to all conquerors past, present, and to come." Since his day an increasing number of artists have unsheathed swords against this ancient enemy of man. Even during World War I, when all the fighting governments commandeered art to help float loans, sustain the Red Cross, and keep up morale, there was discernible an undercurrent of protest at the inhumanity of war. It culminated in the fierce cartoons of Raemaekers the Dutchman who so frequently used the figure of the suffering Christ to teach us that war is aimed not only at political and economic domination but at the destruction of the dearest ideals of humanity. The Second World War has already brought similar denunciations. One of the most powerful is Thomas Benton's *Again* (Plate XIII A), begun the day after Pearl Harbor (December 8, 1941). The crucified Christ hangs in a desolated landscape. Three men, in whose distorted faces we recognize the leaders of the Axis powers, are together thrusting the spear into Christ's side, while a dive bomber is strafing the Cross from above. The painter's caption, as given in *Newsweek* reads:

Jesus Christ has stood through the centuries as the preeminent symbol of the brotherhood of man. Over and over again, evil people mad with dreams of power have driven the centurion's spear into His side. Again . . . the old assault is loosed. Mastery, not brotherhood, control, not sharing, are the slogans of the new attackers.

But the distinctive contribution of art to socialized religion lies in the area of industry and economics, in attacks against materialism, greed, the treatment of racial minorities, the forgotten man. In Alcove B we find first the industrial portraits of Gerrit Beneker (d.1934) which he painted in a steel

PLATE XIII (A)

AGAIN

By Thomas Benton. Painted after Pearl Harbor, December 8, 1941. Courtesy of Associated American Artists and the owner of the picture, Abbott Laboratories

PLATE XIII (B)

HOMECOMING OF THE WORKERS IN THE NEW DAY

By Orozco. Courtesy of the New School for Social Research, New York City

PLATE XIV

THREE FRESCOES BY
QUINQUELA MARTIN,
BUENOS AIRES

(A) Unloading Coal
(B) Departure of Fishermen
(C) Self-Portrait

mill in Cleveland in 1919. Though far from being a church-man, Beneker was the most consciously religious of all these artists. His philosophy he stated in a sentence: "To create character is the highest purpose of art." He set up his studio in the steel mill in the hope that in his portraits he might isolate, and hold up for the workers to see, one facet after another of what he called "coöperative personality"; he tried to dignify in the worker's mind each man's personal contribu-tion—the faithfulness of the elevator man, the rugged loyalty of the truckman, the foreman's power of appraisal tempered with humaneness, the constructive contribution of the rad-ical, justice in *Men Are Square*. Beneker felt that art in general was too high-brow, too divorced from the thrust and drive of life. "Go into any of our museums," he wrote, "and you will find no paintings of American labor. These museums are controlled by old capital in trust, and are directed by old minds of an age that is dying. Let us look forward to the day when labor will employ artists, actors, poets, dramatists, musicians, to sing its ideals and aspirations." Beneker called Art for Art's sake "tricks in paint." He therefore dedicated his talent to the realization of Tolstoi's dream: "The destiny of art is to transmit from the realm of reason to the realm of feeling the truth that the well-being of man consists of being united—living and working together."

Certain contemporary artists are enlivening the exhibi-tions with their insights into social problems. Reginal Marsh calls attention to the effect upon children of adult inhumani-ties in his drawing called *This Is Her First Lynching!* Wil-liam Gropper emotionalizes for us the death sentence passed upon Jews in his *Minorities;* Jacques Martin dramatizes the unfraternal disputes in Labor by his *Trouble in 'Frisco;* Irwin Hoffman stirs us with his picture called *Rubbish*—a derelict youth of the depression days; and Orozco the Mex-ican, in his fresco *The Homecoming of the Workers in the*

*New Day* (Plate XIII B), helps us realize that domestic troubles—nagging, frayed nerves, children's fear of drunken fathers, poor food, impoverished spiritual opportunities, and the slum for a dwelling-place—will be mitigated or abolished in the "New Day," the day when justice is done and when human welfare takes precedence over profits.

These pictures all point in the same direction as the Gospel. Whether or not the artist is conscious of the fact, they are religious.

A final illustration will show the power of art to ennoble life and to inspire youth. In the city of Buenos Aires lives a painter named Quinquela Martin. He began life as an anonymous waif. He tells all he knows about his origin in a single sentence: "A man and a woman came together and out sprang an artist!" The slum on the waterfront was his habitat, but that fact could not stifle his genius. With a piece of coal he sketched the stevedores with whom he worked. He taught himself to paint. He became famous, and for an artist well-to-do. Then instead of moving up into the highbrow world, learning the patter of the esthete and crashing the gates of society, out of his own resources he built a school in the slums where he was born and opened it free to the children of that area. In every room he painted a magnificent mural, glorifying the work the children's fathers were doing —coal-heavers, fishermen, draymen, stevedores—exalting the dignity of the labor which is essential to society (Plate XIV). On the top floor he created a museum of originals and replicas and there placed his own studio, through both of which his pupils can wander at will and watch him work. With the proceeds of his pictures sold to the Tate Gallery of London, the Luxembourg of Paris, and the Metropolitan of New York City, he has just bought an adjacent piece of land on which he plans to erect a trade school where he may educate his boys and girls to become creative citizens.

This is art for Life's sake, the dedication of genius not to the task of producing esthetic thrills but of magnifying those values which give dignity to man and issue as brotherhood. Who shall say that this man's work is not as pure "bhakti" as that of Fra Angelico? It is a love offering to humanity.

We have now come to the end of our Museum. Our view has been most cursory; yet I hope it has conveyed to you a hint of the almost limitless field of religious art, of the indispensable function it has performed in all the religions of mankind, and of the unusual possibilities for religious education it still possesses. Some day, when our Museum actually materializes, it must become the most vital and radiant educational center in any city; for only in some such place can the rich heritage of religious art be saved from oblivion and given a perpetual reincarnation in human life.

# *Bibliography*

Leo Frobenius & Douglas C. Fox: *Prehistoric Rock Pictures in Europe and Africa*. Museum of Modern Art, New York, 1937
The latest short and untechnical summary of the findings in the field indicated. Well illustrated.

E. A. Wallis Budge: *The Gods of the Egyptians*. 2 Vols. London, 1904
The authoritative work, not too technical for laymen. Well illustrated.
————: *The Book of the Dead*. London, 1923
Full introduction, complete translation, and many illustrations.

Ananda Coomaraswamy: *The Dance of Siva*. London, 1918
The philosophy underlying Hindu art. A difficult book, but indispensable.

E. B. Havell: *A Handbook of Indian Art*. London, 1920
A non-technical account of sculpture, painting and architecture, both Hindu and Buddhist.

Laurence Binyon: *Painting in the Far East.* London, 1913
A scholarly but popularly written survey of Chinese and Japanese art, by a recognized British authority.

Ernst Pfuhl: *Masterpieces of Greek Drawing and Painting.* Macmillan, 1926
One hundred sixty admirable reproductions with full description of each.

Gilbert Murray: *Five Stages in Greek Religion.* London, 1930
A penetrating study by a great Oxford scholar.

*Encyclopédie Photographique de l'Art:* Nos. 19–22, Greek Vases. Paris, 1937–1938.
Beautiful reproductions of the collection in the Louvre. Captions in French and English.

Charles R. Morey: *Medieval Art.* Norton, 1942
The latest and most inclusive analysis of this field, from the roots of Christian art in earlier cultures to the end of the Gothic period.

Emile Mâle: *Religious Art In France, XIII Century.* Dutton, 1913
The standard work on medieval iconography and its sources of inspiration. 190 illustrations.

H. R. Willoughby: *The Karahissar Gospels.* 2 Vols. University of Chicago
Facsimile reproductions of the miniatures, together with full historical and cultural data.

Percy Gardner: *The Principles of Christian Art.* Scribner, 1928
A non-technical presentation of the relation of art to religion, and an interpretation of the Christian art of various epochs.

Albert E. Bailey: *Art and Character.* Abingdon-Cokesbury Press, 1938
A statement of the religious values to be found in art, interpretations of many pictures, and a brief survey of the religious art of the Western nations.
————: *The Gospel in Art.* Pilgrim Press, new edition, 1936
The interpretation of over one hundred religious pictures.

# II

# THE EXPRESSION OF RELIGION IN ARCHITECTURE

*By* KENNETH JOHN CONANT

PROFESSOR KENNETH JOHN CONANT, A.B., M.ARCH., PH.D., is Professor of Architecture, in Graduate School of Design, Harvard University. The next year, after securing his Bachelor of Arts degree from Harvard, he began his travels which have taken him to all parts of Europe. He was in France as a member (Captain of Engineers) of the Rainbow Division, A.E.F. In 1927 he was appointed a Guggenheim Fellow for work at Cluny to which he has given much scholarly attention. Since 1920 he has been on the Harvard University staff, and Professor of Architecture since 1936. The following is an incomplete list of his honors and achievements—Research Associate in Archaeology of the Mediaeval Academy of America; member of the editorial board of The Art Bulletin; member of the Managing Committee of the American School of Classical Studies at Athens; Harvard exchange professor at the Sorbonne; also at the National University of Mexico; member American Academy of Arts and Sciences, Société Française d'Archéologie, Academie de Maçon, Academie de Dijon, Chevalier of the Legion of Honor. His doctor's thesis resulted in a book entitled "The Early Architectural History of the Cathedral of Santiago de Compostela." Since 1926 his chief object of research has been the Abbey of Cluny. Research projects have also been prosecuted in Kiev, Russia, and on St. Sophia in Constantinople, as well as in Yucatan and New Mexico.

# II

## THE EXPRESSION OF RELIGION IN ARCHITECTURE

A CENTURY AGO, when our religious world became conscious once more of the greatness of medieval contributions to faith and order in the church, there was a natural revival of interest in the monuments which served as the characteristic setting for medieval religion. In spite of disapproving academicians, men of the seventeenth and eighteenth centuries had felt the picturesque charm of their heritage of medieval architecture. Its greater qualities were understood by a generation of analysts and teachers who arose in the nineteenth century, and they were able by their precept to enlarge the general appreciation of it. The writings of these men are often deeply stamped with religious feeling, and the ultimate result of their work has been a sincere love of medieval architecture, widely diffused among laymen and clergy alike.

This love has been shared by the historians and architects who have carried the study forward on a scientific basis. Their publications do not often have the rhapsodical tone which was natural in the age of romanticism, but they have built up a vast body of knowledge on which an intelligent appreciation may be based. Technicians have developed a system of practice such as is necessary for the maintenance and repair of medieval buildings and for the erection of new buildings in the medieval style. An abundant literature concerned with the many problems of medieval archaeology has come into being, and during the last half-century an accurate and detailed chronology has been set up by the effort of gifted and patient architectural historians. They have been able to trace with certainty the streams of influence whose fecund inter-action brought about continuing structural and stylistic advance. Such studies have also made it clear that many of the most influential and important monuments are no longer in existence. It is a fact that no consecutive history of church architecture can be written without some attention to these lost monuments where the architecture of whole regions, and considerable periods of time, came to a focus in creative designs. Therefore the present generation of architectural historians has worked with the spade, and closely studied the accumulated information on both extant and lost monu-ments, in order to recall the lost monuments to their rightful places.

Writers at present, with their much more extensive data, are able to show that the "Gothic miracle" came as the crown-ing development in a long and ordered process. The Gothic achievement is seen not as a momentary incandescence of spirit, but as the embodiment of architectural thought and ideas worked out over a period of nine centuries. It is the purpose of the present essay to follow this development by studying four critical episodes in the history of church build-ing before the Gothic period. We shall see that each of these episodes brought something essential into the tradition of church building—monumentality, permanence, dramatic composition, and a novel structural unit—thus preparing the way of the Gothic designers who created those ever-memo-rable shrines which our hearts and minds tell us are the most sublime in all religious architecture. The later periods need not concern us here, for the elements which were elaborated in the Renaissance occur in pre-Gothic times, and Gothic architecture itself presents, though in different terms, the basic ideas of modern church architecture.

I

The earliest Christian architecture did not have a style as such. The new community used buildings of ordinary character—houses of various types, more or less transformed to fit them for worship, halls of various sorts, including some resembling mystery temples and basilican synagogues, and funerary meeting places at or below the surface. An archaeologist makes the telling comment that perhaps we have the excavated remains of many churches, unrecognized because they show no specific Christian characteristics. No one of these earliest churches is reported as being particularly substantial or valuable, and no special type is known to have had an established inter-regional prestige. The Christian population of the Roman Empire numbered some five or six millions by the year 300, with perhaps half of it in Asia Minor and the immediate neighborhood. If any type of church building was dominant in that area, it was one which resembled the basilican synagogues of Palestine or the "Hellenistic basilicas" of later times.

Diocletian's decree during the great persecution of 303–304 brought about the destruction of this earliest Christian architecture, but good came out of the catastrophe, for an immense and consistent building programme was undertaken under imperial auspices soon after the Peace of the Church.

When in the sequel Christianity became the imperial religion, its buildings no longer expressed merely the space needs of the local congregations. They had to express something of imperial majesty because the Church had become a recognized organ of imperial society. Constantine was the patron of several important church buildings; the imperial office of works was unquestionably employed on them, and quite naturally the noble traditions of imperial building invested the fabric of the churches with true monumentality.

Here we have the first element of the sublime in architecture.

Several conspicuous Early Christian churches were clearly designed to accommodate congregational worship by the entire Christian contingent of populous cities, which posed a problem on the scale of the grandest civic architecture of Roman times. It is perhaps fair to say that Christianity was the only living and growing thing in the late Empire; consequently its architecture was the only living architecture—the problems of civic and domestic building had already received their solution. With a new monumental type to be developed—a church type magnificent enough to represent the Empire—the Church was bound to be the beneficiary of anything the building art could offer.

Thus it was that in Constantine's reign church architecture became not merely monumental and imperial: it became the premier architecture of the whole Mediterranean basin and vast regions beyond. It retained its preëminence thereafter almost without interruption until the seventeenth century. New problems were oftenest broached in church building, and solutions there achieved were applied in other structures.

From what has been said it will be seen at once that the first notable imperial church, at the head of so illustrious a line, possessed extraordinary historical importance. It has been destroyed, but we fortunately have a great deal of information about it, and the main facts are clear. The key monument of Early Christian architecture was of course the old basilica of St. Peter in the Vatican (Plate XV), built by Constantine and dedicated in the year 326. Though it confessed the calamitous times by use of demolition materials imperfectly matched to one another, its immense size (it was always one of the world's largest churches) and its grand conception were authentically imperial. The elements were Roman, drawn at large from imperial civic and temple archi-

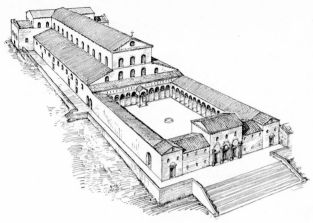

(A) Restored bird's-eye view. The podium and the propylaeum
are in part conjectural (Conant)

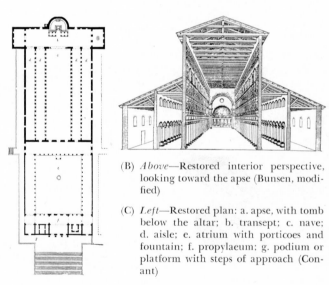

(B) *Above*—Restored interior perspective,
looking toward the apse (Bunsen, modified)

(C) *Left*—Restored plan: a. apse, with tomb
below the altar; b. transept; c. nave;
d. aisle; e. atrium with porticoes and
fountain; f. propylaeum; g. podium or
platform with steps of approach (Conant)

PLATE XV

(A) Restored east view, showing supposed original scheme of great buttresses and dome, later rebuilt (Conant)

(B) *Left*—Reflected plan, showing great dome, hemicycles, and apses of central space, and also the domed cross units of the aisles (Prost)

(C) *Right*—Analytical section showing structural character; dome and buttresses shown as rebuilt, 558–563 A.D. (Prost)

PLATE XVI

tecture, but chosen and ordered according to specifically Christian requirements, so that the result was an unmistakably Christian building. The layout was determined by the tomb of the Apostle, where a magnificent axial development was brought to climax. The pavement level, also settled in reference to the tomb, was somewhat below grade at the head of the composition, but well above the open plaza at the approach end. The entrance system was necessarily elaborate, for it served the church offices and residences as well as the basilica, and had to provide egress for the catechumens during the service. The problem of communication was important, for the church proper would accommodate a standing congregation of about forty thousand people. The whole solution at Old St. Peter's was so masterly that it has been repeated with variations in every subsequent age down to the present, and it is correct to say that this design, where Christian architecture was first declared to the world, was the most influential church design ever composed.

At the side of the open space known as the Campus Sancti Petri rose a splendid flight of steps—familiar of course to the Romans in religious architecture—to a platform on which the frontispiece of the group looked down. In the middle was a propylaeum of the sort which had long been used to provide entrance into important group compositions—religious shrines among them. By Carolingian times, if not before, the propylaeum was flanked by two towers, reminding us of the outer façade of Baalbek in Syria, the grandest Roman temple complex ever built. From the propylaeum hall the visitor to Old St. Peter's entered a noble peristylar atrium. As has been explained, the atrium and the church beyond occupied a terrace, like some of the most magnificent Roman temples (Baalbek among them), but the terrace at Old St. Peter's was functional rather than ostentatious, being required by the level of St. Peter's tomb.

The church nave was one of the noblest interior spaces of antiquity, resembling a splendid consistory or law-court hall (Plate XV C). The central span was about 80 feet, with two 30-foot aisles on either side, above the roofing of which came the vast radiant clearstory windows of the central nave, and at the eaves level, about 120 feet from the pavement, the bearing of the huge timber trusses. In length the nave measured about 295 feet, and the long dimension was emphasized by the tall columnar supports, marshaled in beautiful processional files to either side. The nave and aisles, really pillared wood-roofed corridor-like units on an immense scale, are the structural and esthetic key of the building. Pillared corridor-like units are among the commonest features of Graeco-Roman architecture, usually combined with simple oblong rooms or halls. In Old St. Peter's the halls appear as transverse elements—the propylaeum, and the capacious transept which adjoined the upper end of the nave and aisles. This transept measured about 60 feet in width and 295 feet in length including the recesses at its extremities. An apse opposite the "triumphal arch" of the nave provided seats for the clergy and a monumental setting for the tomb and altar, while at the same time it brought the strong axial movement gracefully to a close. The grand axis measured about 835 feet from end to end, yet the greatness of the building was not merely that of size, and regret was sincere when it was demolished to make way for the church of Bramante, Michelangelo, and Maderna on the same site.

Stock criticisms of the present structure condemn its lightness and cheerful polychrome decoration. But these are inherited from the elder building, and indeed from ancient practice in general. Medieval gloom came into the churches when the attempt was made (as it was in a few cases during late Roman times) to vault the basilica by Roman methods. Judging church architecture as a whole, we may say that the

abundant light and the colorful decoration exemplified in the
Christian Roman basilica have been typical.

## II

The need for large churches throughout the Empire was
so great in Constantine's reign (since his reversal of Diocletian's policy meant new building everywhere) that the basilican type, relatively cheap to build, was a logical choice. Even
the munificence of Constantine had its limits. A similar condition prevailed in the fifth century, when evangelization in
the cities was virtually completed. Cities emptied into the
churches; church capacity had to be doubled and trebled,
and it was natural to continue with the economical wooden-
roofed basilica. But the example of Roman civic architecture
—permanent and fireproof in construction—was everywhere
present. When church architecture became preëminent, it
was inevitable that the churches should be built as permanent
first-class constructions according to the excellent standard
set in fine civic buildings.

The quality of permanence was first achieved for church
architecture in eastern Christendom, by the Byzantine style
created in Constantinople (the former Byzantion). The Byzantines considered, and indeed called themselves Romans—
*Romaioi*—but the creative episode in their architecture began when they gave up heavy Roman vaulting methods and
introduced the thin-shell brick vault of ancient Mesopotamia.
Even more curious is the fact that this half-oriental style
exhibits unmistakable theoretical similarities to Gothic. The
resemblances are technical, not superficial; taken together
they show that new type of building required novel architecture. Byzantine and Gothic both plan for fireproof interiors
with a minimum of heavy pier construction, both sustain
the upper and middle portions of a building on stilt-like
supports, passing the vault-thrusts on to outer portions; both

use a repeating unit-element of structure with corner supports and curtain walls, usually non-supporting window screens; both use thin-web vaulting of double curvature; both employ ribbed and lobed structure, and functional curves are used in both (though not exclusively), instead of the semicircular classical arch. The eye of a specialist is needed to discern these common characteristics because Byzantine and Gothic superstructures differ so much, but the basic relationship is there. Technically the difference comes because the Byzantine architect uses as his basic element the "domed cross unit," in which thrusts are received into a border of four barrel vaults, placed end-on about a domed-up principal vault in the center. This leaves unresolved thrusts in the upper part of the structure. The Gothic architect carries the thrusts of his ribbed groin vaulting to the ground by specially designed buttresses which are recognized in the esthetics of the building as necessary organic parts. The Gothic scheme is the more lucid of the two; it offers the architect greater freedom and greater opportunity, but its purpose was not different from what the Byzantine architects had in mind.

With Byzantine as with Early Christian architecture, the key monument is an imperial church. St. Sophia in Constantinople (Plate XVI A and C) was built by Justinian and dedicated to Christ as the creative Word of God, Holy Wisdom in the Godhead. It is the creative Byzantine building because here the "domed cross unit" was first used in repetition to form the complex of a great design. Four domed cross units appear in each of the lateral aisles and each of the lateral galleries. The seventeenth unit is the marvelous central dome, augmented by a system of hemicycles in order to cover a longitudinal nave. All of the vaults have relatively simple geometry except the main dome, which is like an immense parachute (with the stresses reversed) and one of the earliest examples of ribbed construction on a large

scale (Plate XVI B). The vast central space is singularly beautiful. Its highly articulated vault is carried on four massive
piers, while columns of marble and eight substantial wall-
piers carry the other vaulting and care for thrusts brought
down from the upper parts of the building. The walls form
a series of screens between the wall piers, and are pierced
by a multitude of windows, while 92 windows illuminated
the middle space directly through the tympana and the vaulting.

This building presents one of the finest examples of the
use of light in architecture. It has the abounding brightness
of an Early Christian basilica, handled not in a theatrical
manner, but with unsurpassed subtlety and art. "The Byzantine architect understood light, and used it as one of his
materials," observed Thomas Whittemore, with deep insight.
Our apprehension of the building as a monument of religion
has surely gained from this particular beauty, and many a
visitor has felt the impulse here to meditate on the light of
faith and Intelligence, drawing a parallel which we find in
the touching Byzantine prayer: ". . . Cause the pure light
of the knowledge of thee to shine in our hearts, and open
the eyes of our mind to perceive thy message of good tidings,
. . . for thou, Christ our God, art the Illumination of our
souls and bodies . . ." "One would declare," the historian
Procopius writes, "that the place was not illuminated from
outside by the sun, but that the radiance originated from
within, such is the abundance of light which is shed about
this shrine." Indeed the vault seems to be sustained on suave
and vibrant light (Plate XVII).

The wonderful appearance of ethereal structure was
achieved partly by geometry, with hemicyclical forms building up in lithe curves to the dome, partly by actual thinness
in the vault fabric, and partly by a delicate interior vesture.
Shimmering gold mosaic was laid on the over-arching sur-

faces, and thin sheets of beautifully figured and colored marble cover the supporting masonry.

Furthermore the richly articulated interior form of the church, with its ample flowing surfaces, produces acoustical effects of magical beauty. A single voice calls the building to life everywhere, and choral song flows from vault to vault like an enchanted flood. The sublimity of Byzantine liturgy surely owes something to this characteristic in its ranking cathedral building. Whether filled with song or silence, the material fabric broods over the interior space, and typifies the inward-looking and contemplative character of East-Christian religion in a most beautiful way. No sensitive visitor remains unmoved by its spirituality.

### III

When the muscular paganism of the barbarians was Christianized, their bold imaginative powers were put to the service of church architecture, which with them, as with the late Romans and the Byzantines, became the preëminent architecture. The fact that they transformed church architecture is a true sign that they made Christianity their own, and their special contribution of dramatic composition was as essential as monumentality or permanence in the creation of Gothic sublimity. The development of dramatic composition in occidental architecture cannot be understood from existing monuments. We are dependent on the investigating medievalist—the architectural detective—for our knowledge of its long process, which extended over centuries: from 500 to 1100 A.D. The development went forward largely in the monasteries, where learning and the arts took refuge from the crash of ancient civilization.

The first churches where the new mode was perceptible occur in the time of Justinian. Perhaps it is better to say instead the time of Clovis, under whom the Franks became

PLATE XVII

ST. SOPHIA, İSTANBUL (CONSTANTINOPLE), 532–563 AND LATER

Interior view made before secularization. This view, although distorted, is one of
the most successful of all in giving an impression of the space and light effects
(Sebah and Joaillier)

(A) Monastery of Centula, Later Called St. Riquier, 793–800 A.D.

Two examples of the telescopic *turritus apex* on the church, one on the Chapel of St. Mary (right), and seven other towers. Now destroyed (Conant)

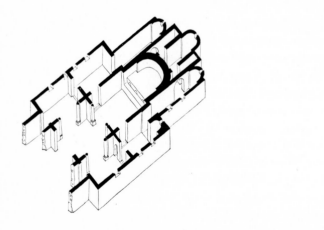

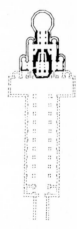

(B) *Left*—St. Philibert de Grandlieu, 814–47 A.D.

The transept (left), sanctuary, and main apse (center) are augmented by an apse echelon. The corridor gave access to the crypt under the main apse (Green)

(C) *Right*—St. Germain, Auxerre

Crypt of 841–51, with angular corridor, apse echelon and rotunda (duodecagon). The nave and transept, on the upper level, are indicated by dotted lines (Conant)

PLATE XVIII

CAROLINGIAN DEVELOPMENTS OF BASILICAN ARCHITECTURE

Christian, for the early examples of which we are informed were built in the area now called France.

The creative step was taken in combining the basilican church with the staged tower or rather *turritus apex,* a spire. Staged towers are known in classic architecture; the Pharos at Alexandria was built many centuries before the first north-European tower forms of which we have report; the late Romans built church towers. But the name *turritus apex* applied by Gregory of Tours (†594) carries a special connotation, and the further development of these tower and pinnacle forms drew on a fund of unmistakably northern taste. In fact through the happy marriage of basilica and *turritus apex* the horizontal, contained, inward-looking and classical church was boldly medievalized through the use of aspiring forms which entirely changed its contour and silhouette.

These emphatic vertical elements were not solely exterior, for lantern towers were common, sometimes with engaging telescopic effects in the upper stages. The belfries and stair turrets were functional, as were the chapels occasionally lodged in the tower-tops. Clearly these elements, though they made the churches conspicuous, were more the result of energy and inventiveness than a mere desire for ostentation, or even dramatic effect alone. In the age of Gregory of Tours the *turritus apex* might be over a lantern tower at the crossing or over a tower-like vestibule, as it was in the noted pilgrimage church of St. Martin in Gregory's own city of Tours. The latter building was perhaps not unlike some of our Georgian churches in general appearance.

By Charlemagne's time the tower and spire motive occurred in much more highly organized compositions. The imperial monastery of Centula or St. Riquier near Abbeville (Plate XVIII A), with dedications in 799 and 800, had, for instance, an atrium with a small tower-chapel over the entrance on each of the three outer sides. The other side was formed by the arched and vaulted vestibule of the church, above which was the imposing mass of an entire spire-church, with lateral stair turrets. Thus was formed one of the most imposing west fronts yet built in church architecture, and since that time we have customarily expected a heavy monumental accent at the entrance façade of an important church building. The interior of the western spire-church of Centula was no less interesting, for it had galleries which were used for an angel choir during the services, and the *turritus apex* was telescopic. The transept had a similar telescopic *turritus apex* and also two lateral stair turrets. There were thus three groups of three towers each, which made the church building a remarkably striking object whether seen nearby or from afar.

Steep roofing in the northern manner also contributed to the dramatic composition of these early medieval buildings. The rapid slope was necessary where, as so often in primitive shelters, poor roofing material was used, or the roof was set on dwarf walls. The convenience of a large roof-space as a loft and its economy of timber with moderate truss spans have perpetuated it, but its use in church architecture is surely due in part to the bold appearance of a great steep roof, and the strong accent of a sharp ridge on a high skyline.

The ninth century saw the French designers at work on dramatic composition in plan as well as in elevation. The greater number of priests among the monastic clergy, for whom the most important building was done, and the multiplying popular relic cults increased the need for minor chapels. Archaeologists have identified remains of many interesting complexes arranged about church sanctuaries—some at crypt level, some semi-subterranean, some at the level of the church pavement. The earlier examples have round or angular passages with an echelon of chapels, and occasionally a rotunda appears on the main axis eastward of the sanctuary (Plate XVIII B and C).

In the tenth century these elements come to have a more intimate relationship with the main apse, particularly through the development (noted at St. Martin of Tours as rebuilt after fires of 903 and 997) of an annular corridor or ambulatory about the apse, looking into it through open arcading, and outward into a regular series of radiating chapels. This motive, when fully understood, was employed to produce wonderfully poetic effects of light and space about the high altars, which were glorified by this beautiful invention.

All of the elements used in plan and superstructure to produce dramatic composition made the actual construction of a church more difficult than before, especially as the monks and their engineers looked to Roman models. Roman engineering was created and developed with very different problems in view, and it was incapable of satisfying the legitimate aspirations of imaginative medieval church builders. We have seen this already in the East, which levied on the orient when its great church style was created. Engineers in the West learned by using Roman forms, and when they had pushed them to the limit, technical skill was such that a radically new structural unit element was invented, specifically applicable to the most highly evolved church designs.

It was eleventh-century Romanesque architecture which realized Roman ideals of fireproof construction for church buildings in the west—heavy structures at the beginning (St. Bénigne, Dijon, 1001–1018 and later), but with continually increasing skill, command, and elegance, in buildings which were often notable for their grand scale as well as for rich sculptural and polychromatic embellishment (Santiago de Compostela, 1078–1124, and many monastic churches).

The first named building had one of the most complex

of all church plans; it was abundant in ideas, not yet so fully controlled and integrated as the ideas of a really great composition must be (Plate XX A). At St. Bénigne there was an eastern axial extension and a central-well rotunda with radiating chapels (these two sections being in three levels) while the third section, a basilica joined on at the west, had an extensive crypt beneath the nave, and galleries above the inner aisles. Thus the nave had three levels also, though not superposed. The plan of the basilica was remarkable for its double aisles flanking both nave and choir and for its interesting combination of ambulatory and apse-echelon (Plate XIX A). The exterior mass, 300 feet long and highly articulated, was broken against the sky by three large towers and six smaller ones. In inventive and dramatic quality this building was more advanced than in its engineering, especially in the nave, where the ponderous supports of the vault were built like an aqueduct or a coliseum. Ultimately they proved intolerable, and the basilica was replaced by a Gothic structure.

In the design of Santiago de Compostela (Plates XIX B, XX B), also planned as a nine-towered church, the old elements were simplified and fused with most admirable art, which makes us regret late-medieval modifications of the exterior and its completion in another style. The original scheme was one of the finest, most representative, and most complete in all the Romanesque, but it was only one in a galaxy of buildings where the medieval gift of dramatic composition was superbly exemplified.

## IV

The late eleventh and the twelfth century demanded great width of span, brilliance of illumination, slenderness of supports, and dynamic composition of church interiors. The early medieval monks for whom Romanesque archi-

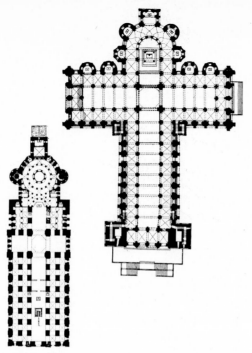

(A) *Left*—St. Bénigne, Dijon, 1001–18 and Later

Original plan. Notable early example of a monastic pilgrimage church, intended to be vaulted completely. The church had nave, aisles, transept, sanctuary with apse, annular corridor, and apse echelon, rotunda, and oblong eastward extension. (By courtesy of the author, Miss Alice Sunderland)

(B) *Right*—Santiago de Compostela, 1078–1140 and Later

Original plan. Notable example of a cathedral pilgrimage church, with fully developed Romanesque plan. The aisles are carried entirely around the nave and transept, appearing about the sanctuary as an annular corridor or ambulatory, with radiating chapels. (Conant)

### PLATE XIX

COMPARISON OF ARCHAIC AND DEVELOPED
ROMANESQUE

(A)—St. Bénigne, Dijon, 1001–18 and Later

Original scheme. Notable combination of vaulted architecture in the Roman manner with dramatic silhouette and highly evolved plan in the Carolingian manner; now destroyed. (By courtesy of Miss Alice Sunderland; Conant drawing, from model made by Miss Elizabeth and Miss Alice Sunderland)

(B)—Santiago de Compostela, 1078–1140 and Later

Original scheme. Towers in part conjectural. A noble ensemble in the fully developed Romanesque style; now much altered on the exterior. (Conant)

PLATE XX

COMPARISON OF ARCHAIC AND DEVELOPED ROMANESQUE

tecture was invented had not been so exigent, for most of the monasteries were in rustic situations or small towns, and much of the monastic liturgy was performed at night. The great pilgrimage churches (of which Santiago was one) stretched Romanesque architecture to its utmost, and a special circumstance posed even greater requirements at the monastery church of Cluny. Romanesque architecture was never intended to supply such floods of light or such oceans of open space as were needed in the ensuing cathedral age, when the greatest religious buildings were built to receive whole cities-full of people at festival time.

The great church at Cluny (1088–1120 and later) (Frontispiece) was almost a match for St. Bénigne at Dijon in elaboration of plan. Greatly improved technique permitted the architect to undertake a span of 32 feet in the clear, with a bold range of clearstory windows under a vault which reached its peak at 99 feet above the pavement. The eastern part of the building, with many apsidal, stepped, intersecting, and tower forms, proved stable. But not the imposing five-aisled nave, built in part for extra altar space, but more especially as a dramatic setting for the Cluniac processional liturgies, which at one of the chapters-general saw as many as 1212 professed monks in line. The 250-foot length of the basilican nave could not safely be built without lateral support. After a partial collapse in 1125 it was repaired and provided with archaic flying buttresses. The narthex, also built for processional reasons, was then added in a primitive Gothic style.

The same problems of lighting and space appeared in the cathedrals. The canons were seated in a much lengthened eastern limb of the cruciform plan (not, like monks, at the head of the nave) in order to liberate the crossing and transepts for the people. Solution of the cathedral problem therefore involved a method whereby the eastern and western arms of the church could be built safely with considerable length, and the crossing made vast and open without obstructive masonry.

In the great Romanesque building at Cluny, as in earlier Byzantine structures, we find premonitions of the Gothic solution of this problem. Pointed arches, approximate catenaries, ribs, thin-web vaulting, and the corner-supported bay with screen window-wall all occurred, but were dispersed here and there in the building, not creatively combined as they were to be in Gothic.

The Gothic style, when fully achieved, possessed a basic unit-element of structure which was applicable everywhere —the typical bay of ribbed groin vaulting. Its supports are slender, planned as stilts to carry the weight only: mutual abutment, spur buttresses, and flying buttresses take care of thrust. The sides of a bay are open arches or screen window-walls. The ribs are slender and logically related to the piers. The arches are normally pointed for easier combination and (through approximation to catenary curves) for diminished internal stress. These members require prepared centering, but the thin light vaulting severies do not, for they bow upwards and are filled arch upon arch until they meet at the level crown. The filling need only be substantial enough to resist if the wooden protecting roof is burned. Such ribbed groin-vaulted bays, many times repeated, make up the entire Gothic building (Plate XXI).

In the narthex at Cluny (c.1130) the designers were groping toward this type of structure. At St. Denis, royal abbey and pantheon, Gothic architecture was really invented (c.1134–44), and it was built on a limited scheme with understanding, at the same time being provided with embellishments in sculpture and stained glass which were forerunners of the greatest Gothic achievements. Perhaps at Laon (c.1160–1205) we have the first assured design which shows a new esthetic fully consonant with the new engineering.

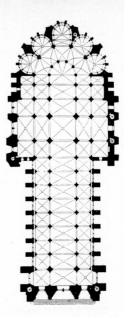

(A) *Left*—West view, with addition of spires—six originally planned, but never built. (Conant)

(B) *Right*—Plan. A perfect Gothic church plan, nobly articulated, beautifully proportioned, and characteristically formed of ribbed groin vault units. (Viollet-le-Duc)

(C) *Right*—View of nave with stained glass removed. This picture shows how the weight of the vault is carried by the ribs to slender trumpet-like supports, while flying buttresses resist any tendency for the vault to tip outwards (i.e., thrust). The flying buttresses rise from the spur buttresses seen on the periphery of the plan, and clear the aisle roofs. (Archives Photographiques)

PLATE XXI

REIMS CATHEDRAL,
1211–85 AND LATER

PLATE XXII

BEAUVAIS CATHEDRAL: THE SANCTUARY

The boldest and most inspiring of Gothic churches (Neurdein)

The nave of Notre Dame in Paris (c.1180–1205) was the first to have assured lateral support by flying buttresses planned integrally from the beginning, and here the height (107 feet to the crown) exceeded that of Cluny for the first time. More logical and complete, though still with lingering traces of archaism, is Chartres (1194). Here a Gothic nave first reached the height of the vaulted Basilica of Constantine in Rome (120 feet) but the 83-foot span there remained out of reach: the usual wide spans in Gothic are about 40 feet; the widest, at Gerona, is 74 feet. Beauvais with 157 feet to the crown of the vault (1227–1325) surpasses the highest Roman vault (the Pantheon, 142½ feet) but not St. Sophia (185 feet), though from 1569 to 1573 the cathedral at Beauvais possessed a phenomenal telescopic vaulted crossing tower —veritable Gothic *turritus apex*—which was 501 feet high. It ought to be said, however, that the majesty of these medieval buildings goes utterly beyond dimension. They offer effects of light, perspective, color, and acoustics which are hardly to be surpassed. This breath-taking development was possible because the logic of Gothic engineering was perfect, because the available stone was admirable for the purpose, and because the masons and carvers had an understanding and skill which is almost past belief.

\* \* \* \*

When the technical stage marked by Chartres had been reached, and the heart-warming beauty of its interior design given to the world, there ensued such a surge of sublime architecture as the world had never seen. Monumentality, permanence, and dramatic composition belonged to the new cathedral buildings by inheritance. The new structural element gave them an unequaled unity. This element in its perfection had not only new freedom, but a new esthetic potentiality which answered one of the most constant desires of the medieval architects. Since the fifth century these men had sought the vertical by repeated emphasis on aspiring forms. Those features were at first exterior, and were only in special cases effective from within as vertical elements. Later the interior proportions and membering developed an unmistakable trend toward verticality. The new engineering made it possible for the Gothic architect to infuse a sweeping dynamic verticality into almost every structural and decorative line of an entire building.

Thus it was that the West-Christian quest in aspiration reached true sublimity. The great surge of cathedral building continued from Chartres, superbly human, to Reims, exact in its perfection and austere as a theological statement by the contemporary St. Thomas Aquinas. Thence it moved to the surpassing airy grace of Amiens and the inspired unutterable loveliness of Beauvais (Plate XXII). No one can look at any one of these noble shrines, the gorgeous crown of nine centuries of aspiration, without deep thankfulness that the hand of man has raised to the spirit of God so glorious a temple.

## Bibliography

Francis Bond: *Gothic Architecture in England.* Batsford, 1906
  Inclusive and authoritative work, giving the background of Gothic in England, as well as the Gothic monuments themselves, with many illustrations.

David Roden Buxton: *Russian Mediaeval Architecture.* Cambridge University Press, 1934
  Convenient and well illustrated volume which has proved useful to all students of the subject.

Alfred W. Clapham: *Romanesque Architecture in Western Europe.* Oxford, Clarendon Press, 1936
  Authoritative presentation by one of the best English architectural historians; in small compass but readable and well illustrated.

Kenneth John Conant: *A Brief Commentary on Early Mediaeval Church Architecture, with Especial Reference to Lost Monuments.* The Johns Hopkins Press, 1942
Self-explanatory title; many illustrations.

Arthur Gardner: *An Introduction to French Church Architecture.* Macmillan, 1938
A short general text, plus tabloid monographs, one with each of the many and systematically chosen illustrations. A good book.

J. Arnott Hamilton: *Byzantine Architecture and Decoration.* Batsford, 1933.
Comprehensive and abundantly illustrated; includes derivative Byzantine work in Russia, the Balkans, Armenia and the West.

Violet R. Markham: *Romanesque France.* Dutton, 1929
Abounds in interesting descriptive and biographical material, but the archaeological material is somewhat subject to caution.

Rexford Newcomb: *Outlines of the History of Architecture,* especially parts II (1932) and IV. Wiley, 1934
Analyses, lists, topographical material, information on materials and engineering problems.

Elizabeth Boyle O'Reilly: *How France Built Her Cathedrals.* Harper, 1921
Vivacious and informative presentation, not overloaded with archaeological items.

Arthur Kingsley Porter: *Medieval Architecture—Its Origin and Development.* Baker and Taylor, 1909
An early work of the eminent medievalist, and in some ways to be used with caution, but notable for a polyglot bibliography and a long series of short descriptive notes on the monuments.

Sartell Prentice: *The Heritage of the Cathedral.* Morrow, 1936
An enthusiastic book with popular appeal, but marred by many sections which appear unsound to a careful historian.

Ernest H. Short: *The House of God.* Macmillan, 1926
A substantial volume treating the great architecture of the several important religions from antiquity to the present; somewhat encyclopaedic in its manner, it nevertheless reads easily, and is fairly dependable.

# III

# THE EXPRESSION OF RELIGION
# IN MUSIC

*By* HENRY AUGUSTINE SMITH

DR. HENRY AUGUSTINE SMITH, a pioneer in the field of church music, has for some years been a national figure. Since his graduation from North Central College, Illinois, he has become well known to American church musicians. His teaching activities have been carried on in two institutions mainly, the Chicago Theological Seminary and Boston University, where he now is head of the Department of Sacred Music. He has been called upon to develop the musical programs in many national and international assemblies, such as the Methodist Centenary (1919), the World Sunday School Convention (1920), the General Assembly of the Presbyterian Church (1920), the International Convention of Religious Education (1922), the International B.Y.P.U. (1929), the Ecumenical Conference of the Methodist Church (1931), and many others. He is equally well-known as editor of Church Hymnals, especially those published by D. Appleton-Century Co. Among these are The Century Hymnal, The Hymnal for American Youth, The New Hymnal for American Youth, and The New Church Hymnal. For several years he was the Director of Music at the Chautauqua Assembly.

# III

## THE EXPRESSION OF RELIGION IN MUSIC

THE STUDY OF CHURCH MUSIC opens up many vistas. Foremost is her glorious history, beginning with Hebrew cantellation, moving forward to the early Christians with their *Glorias* and *Misereres,* on to Rome and the *Schola Cantorum,* side-stepping to include the quasi-religious troubadours and minnesingers, culminating in the polyphony of Palestrina, capturing warmth and democratic character in the chorales of Luther and his co-workers, acquiring severity through John Calvin and Psalm-singing Scotland, gaining further impetus through Anglican chant and Tudor anthems, and achieving supreme heights and profound character in the writings of John Sebastian Bach and Georg Friedrich Handel, with the organ finally breaking through as the accepted church instrument.

Continuing the march of sacred music up the centuries, the Wesley singing societies swing into action as also Isaac Watts, father of the English hymn, followed by American church song, sired by William Billings, Lowell Mason, and a trio of discerning clergymen, on to the Oxford movement and the Victorian era, and to the lay evangelism of Moody and Sankey as a counteractive, and lastly to the renaissance of church music schools and multiple choirs during the past forty years.

To many worshipers, this art is none other than the pipe organ, filling the front of the sanctuary with its golden pipes; with its orchestral colors flooding every niche and cranny of God's house and holding human hearts in thrall.

. . . When beneath the nave,
High arching, the cathedral organ 'gins
Its prelude, lingeringly exquisite
Within, retired, the bashful sweetness dwells;
Anon like sunlight, or the flood-gate rush
Of waters, bursts it forth; clear, solemn, full,
It breaks upon the mazy-fretted roof;
It coils up round the clustering pillars tall;
It leaps into the cell-like chapels; strikes
Beneath the pavement sepulchres; at once
The living temple is instinct, ablaze
With the uncontrolled exuberance of sound.[1]

The picture changes: behold white-robed choristers in traditional vestments marching on wings of song to loft, gallery, or chancel; singers recruited from neighborhood homes and far-flung parish life, ages seven to seventy. Mayhap a quartet is in vogue, enrapport, through their heightened personalities, with the music committee.

Church song with the clergy is largely congregational participation, good or bad, a flare-up of robust tone on old favorites or a silent revolt against all new words and song settings, nevertheless a futile or successful attempt at worship through people's song.

Music as the child of the church owes her very existence through the dark ages, her housing in abbey, chapel and cathedral, her immortal themes from Holy Scriptures and her evolution as a tonal language, to ecclesiastical officers and laymen in refectory and monastery, and on missionary pilgrimages. Through sixteen hundred years, her grammar and rhetoric, her literature, her educational system, her territorial expansion, her laws and doctrines and momentum, her executives, schoolmasters, composers, performers, devotees, and students have come up through the church.

---

[1] Henry Hart Milman: "The Pipe Organ in the Cathedral."

While this tonal art is the child of religion, Mother Church on the other hand is in incalculable debt to her daughter, for have not the Psalms, for example, evolved in content, structural form, and liturgic usefulness, largely because of their musical settings, their processional make-up, their antiphonal character; a worship and festival book grounded on abundant and variegated music settings?

Note Psalm 107 as a pendulum swing between God's blessing on, and his punishment of, his people; with a major and a minor chorus punctuating the crescendos and diminuendos:

*Cantor: ff* O give thanks unto the Lord, for he is good;
for his mercy endureth forever.
Let the redeemed of the Lord say so,
whom he hath redeemed from the hand of the enemy;
And gathered them out of the lands, from the east,
and from the west, from the north, and from the south.
 *dim* They wandered in the wilderness in a solitary way;
they found no city to dwell in.
Hungry and thirsty, their soul fainted in them.

*2d Choir:* Then they cried unto the Lord in their trouble,
 *cres* and he delivered them out of their distresses.

*Cantor:* And he led them forth by the right way,
 *cres* that they might go to a city of habitation.

*1st Choir:* O that men would praise the Lord for his goodness,
 *cres* and for his wonderful works to the children of men.

*Cantor: ff* For he satisfieth the longing soul,
and filleth the hungry soul with goodness.
 *dim* Such as sit in darkness and in the shadow of death,
being bound in affliction and iron;
Because they rebelled against the words of God,
and contemned the counsel of the Most High:
Therefore he brought down their heart with labor;
 *pp* They fell down, and there was none to help.

*2d Choir*: Then they cried unto the Lord in their trouble,
 *cres* and he saved them out of their distresses.

*Cantor:* He brought them out of darkness and the shadow of death,
 *cres* and break their bands asunder.

*1st Choir:* O that men would praise the Lord for his goodness,
 *cres* and for his wonderful works to the children of men.

*Cantor: ff* For he hath broken the gates of brass,
 and cut the bars of iron in sunder!

This and other antiphonal Psalms await transcendent musical settings. Arise, musicians, and strike your lyre:

> Let your silver chime
> Move in melodius time;
> And let the bass of heaven's deep organ blow;
> And with your ninefold harmony
> Make up full consort to the angelic symphony! [2]

Music as the handmaid of religion is further evidenced by the half-million lyrics, intoned, carolled, hymned; stretching from Clement of Alexandria in the third century to the 1940 hymns of Bland Tucker and Bishop Spencer. The immortal music settings of the Mass by Mozart, Bach, and Beethoven have familiarized both Catholic and Protestant alike with the inviolate acts of worship as powered by the *Kyrie* and *Gloria in Excelsis,* the *Sanctus* and *Benedictus,* the *Credo* and *Agnus Dei,* while the oratorios of Heinrich Schütz, Haydn, Handel, and Mendelssohn have illumined the Bible pictorially and dramatically for millions through their settings of the *Seven Words from the Cross,* the *Creation, Elijah, St. Paul,* and the *Messiah.*

At the outset there is to be noted a differentiation between religious and church music, for the latter has a style all its

---

[2] John Milton: *Ode on the Morning of Christ's Nativity.*

own, distinct from secular and religious. Religious music may include all music with sacred words; florid, dramatic and virtuoso styles; oratorio, cantata, motet and passion music, too extended and technical for the church service.

Organ repertoire too often favors the andantino, berceuse, meditation, march pontificale, and fanfare, reminiscent of *Thaïs, Tannhaüser, Tales of Hoffman, Cavalleria Rusticana,* and *Hansel and Gretel,* and such orchestral suites as *Peer Gynt No. 1, L'Arlesienne,* and *Sylvia.* Such music becomes religious only through time and place, and up to the moment when previous musical experiences and circumstances of hearing are bound to play havoc with worship. The organ should at all times have tonal beauty and strength, and create elevation of spirit and state of mind where worship is easy and immediate.

Anthems and cantatas continue to pour forth at flood tide with sensuous melodies, candied harmonies, and rhythms that step up heart beats. They are heartily accepted, cherished, fought for, so long as they are "what one likes"—not how good and great is the Lord God, but how good this music makes one feel. Much of the vocal and instrumental music as performed in the sanctuary today is not churchly, but secular even with Biblical texts.

Is there sacred music as such, in its structural form? Has music inherent moral character? Is it more emphatically on the side of right than of wrong?

This art has not always been in clean hands and come from pure hearts. It will, in control of an unchaste spirit, drown human life in the deepest sea.

Amos condemned music:

> Take away from me the noise of thy songs,
> For I will not hear the melody of thy viols.

Moffatt translation:

> No more of your hymns for me!
> I will not listen to your flutes.[3]

These degenerate musicians stain the pages of history: Dionysius the Younger, master of Syracuse in the fourth century B.C., the Ptolomies and Cleopatra, and Nero, who believed himself an accomplished artist and accepted princely fees for his singing and fiddling. There was Heliogabolus, Roman emperor at the age of sixteen, a flute player, who lured youth through oriental naturalistic religion and amorous music into grossest sensual pleasures.

Plato protested against the use of Lydian and Ionian melodies: "Sweet and soft airs may temper the spirit like steel, but if one carries on the softening and soothing process, in the next stage he begins to melt and waste, until he has wasted away his spirit, and cut out the sinews of his soul and he becomes a feeble warrior." [4]

Augustine feared that the "sweetness of music might beguile his soul and make him forget the words." Chrysostom warned that all music should be grave and solemn, not theatrical.

Quakers protested vehemently: "Music produces an excitement mistaken for devotion, and makes entertainment of the most awful events recorded in Holy Scriptures." An example of this is Rossini's setting of the *Stabat Mater Dolorosa,* and in particular his trumpet blast for tenor, coupled with infectious marching rhythms and orgy of high notes: *Cujus animam.* Tears of sorrow for the weeping mother at the cross should have chastened this musical utterance:

---

[3] *The Holy Bible,* translation by James Moffatt.
[4] *The Republic of Plato,* translated by Davies and Vaughan.

Through her heart, his sorrow sharing,
And his bitter anguish bearing,
Now at length the sword has passed.

Is not the sorrowing Mary a symbol of universal motherhood as never before?—the sword piercing through many a mother's heart whose son is reported as "missing in action."

Even Handel in his lighter moments took two of his earlier love songs and transferred them to his Messiah score: "For unto us a Child is born" and "All we like sheep have gone astray." Cowper might well protest:

Ten thousand sit
Presently patient at a sacred song,
Commemoration mad, content to hear——
O wonderful effect of music's power——
Messiah's eulogy for Handel's sake.

Prior to Cowper's day, Lavington, in 1731, preached a sermon in which he uttered this warning:

Music is a two-edged sword; capable of quelling the passions, so of giving mortal wound to virtue and religion; and therefore should always be in sober hands. . . . Quick and powerful, and penetrating the minutest parts of the body, and inmost recesses of the spirit, when employed under the banner of religion; but likewise searching and irritating every evil thought, and intention of the heart, when debauched in the service of immorality and profaneness. What ought to kindle a devout affection, may blow up every evil desire into a flame, may be the fuel and incentive for vice.[5]

Out of this debacle of tonal art, often in the guise of religion, there arises absolute church music, definitely worshipful in its structural form: melody, scales, harmony, counterpoint, rhythm, and tempo; joined to the Bible and to extra-Biblical material, and to the acts of worship.

---

[5] Archibald Davison: *Protestant Church Music in America.*

Music is different from the sister arts in that it arouses "as many different ideas as there are listeners." The Victory theme from Beethoven's *Fifth Symphony* may mean fate knocking at the door, or the composer's tragic loss of hearing, or his violent attachment for one of his pupils, or the call of the yellow-hammer. Quiet music may be the gentle motion of the sea, the wind in the tree tops, romance under moonlit skies, or an investigator in silent search after ultimate truth.

## I. Tonal Structure

While music is largely dependent upon words, on time and place, on tradition and association, it does assume stature as church music *per se*.

1. The MELODY or tune should be simple, limited in range and not scampering all over the chord outline; austere and impersonal, and not attracting attention to itself; not too obvious a pattern, repeated over and over, as in "Three Blind Mice" and "Over There." It should moreover be free from languishing sharps and flats, diminished and augmented intervals, particularly the innocuous diminished seventh. Among tunes having stamina and elevation, singable withal, are the Plainsong melodies, *Divinum Mysterium, Alla Trinita Beata,* and *Veni Emmanuel;* the French and German chorales, *Old Hundredth, Coelites Plaudant, Lasst uns Erfreuen, Lobe den Herren,* and *Nun Danket alle Gott;* and these English tunes, ranging through four hundred years: *Tallis' Canon, St. Anne, St. Thomas, Duke Street, Rockingham, Hanover* and *Sine Nomine.*

Melody (and harmony) are bidding for church sanction today, founded not alone on major and minor scales, but upon the eight modal scales of Bishop Ambrose of Milan, fourth century, and Gregory the Great, sixth century:

| | |
|---|---|
| The Dorian Mode | from D to D (white keys of the pianoforte) |
| The Hypodorian | A to A |
| The Phrygian | E to E |
| The Hypophrygian | B to B |
| The Lydian | F to F |
| The Hypolydian | C to C |
| The Mixolydian | G to G |
| The Hypomixolydian | D to D |

and an additional mode of later origin, *Tonus Peregrinus* (The Pilgrim tone).

These modal scales are preëminent church music, having the feel of a cathedral, the beatific light through clearstory windows, the lift of the nave, and the artistry of transcepts.

The Eastern or Byzantine church has fostered another scale (C, D flat, E, F, G, A flat, B, and C) plus the modal patterns heretofore listed. For eleven hundred years, dating from John of Damascus, eighth century, Greek and Russian church musical art lay hidden away, undiscovered, until Andrew White, minister to Russia from 1892 to 1894, George Frederick Wright of Oberlin, and Count von Moltke of Germany, hearing for the first time the choir of the Imperial Chapel at St. Petersburg, one hundred and twenty boys and men, wrote glowing accounts of this transcendent choral song, with not an instrument anywhere, any time; only male voices, with *sub bassos* singing foundation tones an octave deeper than the normal bass, with rhythm ranging from funereal pace to staccato and whirlwind speed, and voices compassing three octaves, as limitless as the Russian steppes.

For one hundred and fifty years, Russia's mighty men of tone have poured forth cherubic hymns and liturgical chants to enrich the Eucharist: Bortniansky, Glinka, Kastalsky, Tschesnokoff, Ippolitof-Ivanoff, Rachmaninoff, Tschaikowsky, and the living Gretchaninoff.

2. HARMONY and 3. COUNTERPOINT are the second and

third media in the building of ecclesiastical tonal structure. The one should consist of simple triads, with a minimum of accidentals. Handel's *Hallelujah Chorus* contains fifteen hundred sung notes. Hold it up to the light: not one sharp nor flat mars its transparent beauty and sublimity!

Counterpoint consists of melodies moving in a horizontal direction, weaving and interweaving, each voice part important in itself, and not dependent as in harmony, on a single melody supported by vertical chords (monodic). This is polyphony (many voices), unquestionably the purest, most spiritual style of choral writing for the sanctuary; however, like Bach's organ and choral literature, it has suffered from discoloration, muddiness in the inner parts, rigid rhythm, and defeatism in the final cadences.

Persistent is the prejudice against minor harmonies. It was once affirmed that while major tonalities increase respiration and stimulate the heart, the minor do just the opposite. The neurotic is depressed, devastated by them. Such deductions fall with a sickening thud in the presence of Cesar Franck's *D Minor Symphony* which is full of noble beauty and arousement bordering on delirium. Both Beethoven's and Brahms' symphonies in C minor stress hard, pitiless struggle, but they do break away into "steely energy and dramatic intensity," with the finale carrying one away on floods of orchestral tone, robust, captivating, triumphant.

Minor tunes are flowing deep and full through many a hymnal, such as *Aberystwyth, Ton-Y-Botel, Llangloffan, Leoni* (Yigdal), a Hebrew melody, and *God rest you merry, gentlemen.*

4. RHYTHM, fourth in the warp and woof of tonal texture, is recurring accent, and accent is bodily vigor. It is musical childhood and adolescence, the inescapable mark of radio bands, jute boxes, movie orchestras, and the dance floor. Its invasion of parish life through the Church School and evan-

gelistic campaigns, has changed sensitive, worshiping souls
into steaming humans, quivering with physical urges, introspective goings on, social pleasantries. For such, surely "God
must be on a journey, or peradventure he sleepeth."

Free rhythm, a better-behaved child than inexorable accent, broke upon an unsuspecting world when last fall the
1940 edition of the Episcopal Hymnal was launched, with no
measure sign in any of its six hundred tunes. Division of
music into bars separated by vertical lines was originally
printed for beginners only. Actors and speakers do not accent
lines with machine-like regularity. So singing and playing
should be flexible. In reading a poem, scansion is secondary,
declamation primary. One must speak the voice, likewise
must one sing the words and mould the music phrases. One
denomination at least will start singing all over again, from
re-created hymn books, free from swinging and marching patterns, with tunes re-edited to bring primary accent of word
and tune together, elongating chords here and there to care
for important nouns, verbs, adjectives, and silent at places
to catch breath, and sense extraordinary meanings just
sung.

The apathy of laymen toward singing is frequently due to
the impossible wedding of sense and sound. What erratic
practice and tradition have put together, the will of the
American church-goer should put asunder. Many a noble text
is torn asunder or entirely submerged by riveting accents or
mountebank skipping. Following are tune examples of accents on unimportant words and on blank spots, or a rush
past God and things eternal as if charioteering to a Roman
holiday.

"O love that wilt not let me go" is a lyric with 132 words,
112 of which are monosyllables such as love, light, joy, cross,
torch. Singing this to the accepted tune, *St. Margaret,* which
abounds in short, snappy eighth notes, is like tumble weed

driven before the wind, whereas the poem itself is drenched in quiet, disciplined, consecrated living.

"O worship the King, all glorious above," on the other hand, is crowded with two- and three-syllable words, and therefore, whether sung to *Hanover* or *Lyons,* should move majestically, and pause anon for orotund sound and resounding phrases. "Power," "defender," "ancient of days," "pavilioned in splendor," "girded with praise," call for strength of voice, length of word, and grandiose movement.

"Holy, holy, holy, Lord God Almighty" is more often "hully" or "hollay" when marching choirs stamp upon it. Sung thus: "Ho-ly (pause), ho-ly (pause), ho-ly (pause)," each one growing in volume, should transform these lines into upward spirals of Hebraic incense, the song impulse for the holy of holies.

The utter disregard for key words, their mispronunciation and misinterpretation, is nowhere more clearly shown than in "These things shall be, a loftier race," where "unarmed" is sung for "inarmed" (arm in arm). "Unarmed" means a third world war; "inarmed" is a guarantee of lasting peace:

> Nation with nation, land with land,
> Inarmed shall live as comrades free.

Schleiermacher affirms: "There is much discussion as to how one can again revive the common expression of the religious life; but it scarcely occurs to anyone that the best results could most easily be achieved if one would again place the song in a more correct relation to the word. What the word has clarified, the tone must vivify, must transport straightway as a harmony into the inner recesses of one's being, and there must hold it fast." [6]

5. Finally TEMPO or pace is the fifth deciding factor as to

---

[6] Schleiermacher: *Die Weihnachtsfeier.*

whether music shall be churchly, religious or merely secular. Tempo is hidden away among the notes of chorales, anthems and hymns, and only the discerning may conjure out of them prayer and praise. "Tempo! that is interpretation," exclaimed Wagner; and Grieg: "A musician who plays too fast or too slowly is sure to bungle all the other intentions of the composer. He shows a lack of what might be called musical instinct." The Italian terms for relative speeds are, by literal translation, moods which should guide in interpretation: *allegro* meaning cheerful, *adagio*—easy, *andante*—going, and *largo*—broad.

A knowledge of the Liturgy of St. Basil and St. Chrysostom, the Byzantine rite, is imperative if the changes in pace and power, the strategy of silence, the subdued intoning, and the exultant choral strophes, are to be factual and vital interpretations of the *Cherubim Hymn,* so strikingly set to music by many a Russian composer:

Let us, the Cherubim mystically representing,
and unto the life-giving Trinity
the thrice-holy chant intoning,
all cares terrestrial now lay aside. *Amen*

### The Great Entrance

That we may raise on high the King of all,
like Conqueror on shield and spears,
by the Angelic Hosts invisibly upborne. *Alleluia.*

Whether Russian or Protestant choir sings, it merits the most expressive tonal colors: uncommonly soft and slow during the Office of Oblation, as an accompaniment to the piercing of the altar breads by a spear, the filling of the Chalice, with censings, ablutions and genuflections. Follows a long-drawn-out *Amen,* which is broken by an intense and jubilant allegro, for is not the Christ present in the flesh! Alleluia!

## II. Expression

From this five-point structure of absolute church music we move to the second life-giving element—that of EXPRESSION. Here the liturgic and non-liturgic churches move their respective ways. The Jew, the Catholic, the Anglican, and the Lutheran view music as an integral part of the liturgy, not detached therefrom. The advantage of repeating the acts of worship Sunday after Sunday, and in the same order, is obvious; for whether music and words are intelligible or not, the steps in the soul's awakening are unchanged. Moreover the architectural setting is such that the worshiper is instanter in the presence of Divinity. The main aisle of chapel, sanctuary, or cathedral, is the pathway to God, down which millions of communicants have streamed through the centuries; through central door of the narthex, under nave, past transcepts, through to the chancel and the high altar. No minister blocks the approaches with a centered pulpit, no choir rises tier on tier to black out this visual center. Always the pathway is step upon step (seven of them) to the Presence, to transactions with God. Lift the communion table to the place of the high altar, and the effect is much the same for disbelievers in high church practices. This focal center, this holy place, should change a morning congregation from hearts filled with distractions, inventories of individual experiences through the past week, feelings intent on music's enjoyment, hearts warmed by social contacts, into united contemplation of, and communion with, their Lord and Master.

The non-liturgic viewpoint treats music as merely accessory. The clergy are trained as prophets and shepherds, not as priests. Music is not the suffuser of worship, but rather a filler-in of awkward voids, a background for last minute errands, the seating of late-comers. On the bulletins appear the names of choirmaster, organist, soloists and choirs participating. Of what moment is a name, a person, a random choral selection and its composer? God is a Spirit and they that worship him, must worship him in spirit and in truth. So all musicians should sing in self-effacing tonal beauty and unction. Protestantism is in dire need of the submerging of personalities.

How shall music, as an expressive force, best serve those free churches that are moving toward patterns of worship such as: 1. Vision or Awareness of God; 2. Vitality or Exaltation; 3. Humility or Confession; 4. Illumination or Instruction; and 5. Dedication or Consecration?

1st Act. The pipe organ is as near the voice of God as any known instrument, beginning with the first chords softly, almost imperceptibly, so that communicants may "feel even before hearing it." Nothing familiar nor reminiscent, nothing displayful nor technical, will sound; rather adagios, elevations, chorales, invocations, or improvisations, restrained in color and sure of registers.

The processional is a questionable act of worship and should be used only on festival occasions. It is too physical, too entertaining for eyes and ears of on-lookers, too muddling in movement and seeking after assigned stalls, too lacking in mystery, to be more than a transfer of a vested unit from one place to another. There are exceptions but not many.

Better that an *introit* or *antiphon* should sound, minister and choir, or choir and congregation, as for example this from the Lutheran church year:

*Minister:* Daughter of Zion: behold thy salvation cometh.
The Lord shall cause his glorious voice to be heard:
and ye shall have gladness of heart.
*Choir:* Give ear, O Shepherd of Israel:
Thou that leadest Joseph like a flock.
Out of Zion, the perfection of beauty, God hath shined:
Our God shall come.

*Minister:* Gather thy saints together unto me:
          Let us go into the house of the Lord.
   *Choir:* Alleluia.
*Minister:* I was glad when they said unto me:
          Let us go into the house of the Lord.
   *Choir:* Our feet shall stand within thy gates, O Jerusalem.
          Alleluia!

2D ACT. Joy, adoration, exaltation are seldom voiced through triumphant song and speech in churches today. The first hymn should fairly blaze with tone, such as:

"Joy to the world, the Lord is come" (an all-year hymn)
"Let all the world in every corner sing"
"Rejoice, ye pure in heart"
"Praise to the Lord, the Almighty, the King of Creation"

Immediately follows the Responsive Reading, lifted out of its mumbling, distraught status into the voice of a great multitude, by singing and speech choirs taking strong leadership. Follows the *Gloria Patri,* beginning softly as reminiscent of its origin in the second century A.D. and rising to impressive power for "is now, and ever shall be, world without end." The voice of ecstasy continues in the first choir anthem, short, sonorous, without solos or long organ passages, as for example:

"With a voice of singing"—Shaw
"O sing unto the Lord" (abridged)—Purcell
"Sing alleluia forth"—Thiman
"*Benedictus es Domine*"—any setting

Transposing of keys within the anthem itself, as in Titcomb's plainsong setting for Easter: "Come, ye faithful, raise the strain" may achieve a moment of sublimity akin to the Elevation of Host and Chalice, ecstatic singing, rising to heaven's very portals!

3D ACT. Humility or confession, the act of the bowed head and repentant heart, has in all lands, ages and tongues, been the one choral prayer of Christendom:

> In English: "O Lord, have mercy upon us"
> In Greek: *"Kyrie, eleison, Christe, eleison"*
> In Latin: *"Miserere nobis"* or *"Miserere Domine"*
> In Russian: *"Gospodi pomolui"*

This choral prayer for mercy and forgiveness should be followed by the General Confession and a Litany or a subjective, experiential hymn of which there are legion.

4TH ACT. Up to this point, the portals of the sanctuary have been wide open for the tripartite patterns of Awareness of God, Exaltation, and Confession of Sin. The next act, that of Illumination or Instruction, a more rational and sagacious mood, swings the portals to, narrowing the attention on doctrine and on sermonic subject-matter as voiced through Scripture, Pastoral Prayer, and the second anthem and the second hymn; for worship includes not alone the "tapping of the magazines of feeling," but indoctrinating the faithful. "The twin arts of poetry and song are an emotional response to doctrine, giving it beauty and grace," observes Dr. Benson. This should explain a certain Unitarian's exclamation on hearing Gretchaninoff's stupendous setting of the Nicene creed: "I believe!" Enraptured song transcends dogma. It is love, not faith, in search of transforming music. "Many who falter are concerned with the outworks, not the citadel."

The second choir anthem, on the theme of Scripture and sermon, will have directness of appeal and hortatory content, such as:

> "God so loved the word"—Stainer
> "Beloved, let us love one another"—Foote
> "Ho, every one that thirsteth"—Martin

5TH ACT. Dedication or consecration, following the sermon, is the offertory, expanded to include not alone pledges and gifts, but forthright surrender of each and every heart to God. No distracting soloists will sally forth to sing, no choral group will intrude to the danger point of entertainment or excellence of performance; only the organ may provide the tonal urge for the consummation of a surrendered life: "Receive, O Lord, these our offerings, and accept with them our hearts and lives, which we do here consecrate to thee. Amen;" climaxed by the Doxology.

### III. MASTERS AND SCHOOLS

For a further study of music as an expressive force, we now turn to the immortal masters and schools of church music, with observations made primarily to correct and stabilize the divine art in this year of our Lord.

Reverting to Hebrew music, we note its crudity, its bald unisons, its blatant trumpets and twanging strings, the tintinnabulation and thumping of its tambours. It achieved no distinction as art, as a tonal language, as something strong and beautiful in itself, being subservient to dramatic recitation delivered in musical tone. Ritual and ceremonial, and these alone, lifted it into noble and impassioned utterance, inciting to the awe of Jehovah, adorning His courts, and transferring to the people directly visions and reproofs of prophets and songsters. Precise timing is to be noted: "When the trumpeters and singers were as one, a cloud filled the temple of the Eternal, so densely, that the priests could not stand to serve. The Eternal's splendor of glory filled the temple of God." [7]

Hebrew music has continued as a national, ethnologic, pictorial language. Especially the recent Psalm settings by

---

[7] *The Holy Bible*, translation by James Moffat. 2 Chronicles 5:13, 14.

Ivor Stravinsky for chorus and orchestra, as heard by the writer, which the composer declared were contrapuntal, pure tone fabrication, and not travestied by reading into them what is not there in substance, voice widest human experience, the largest reaches of the human mind, the pathos of a shattered race, the deepest valleys and highest peaks of Israelite wanderings in all lands. How may one better understand the rhapsodic lines of melody, decorative etchings, and *portamentos,* except as tonal longings for freedom and deliverance from persecution and death? Hebrew music is, first and last, racial, biographic, festival.

Two church music schools, sole originators and arbiters of scales, techniques, expressional devices through fifteen hundred years, came into being to voice the mystery of the Presence, the dramatization of the Lord's Supper, the Mass of the Catholic Church. Gregory the Great through his *Schola Cantorum* at Rome set the irrevocable patterns of church music along the lines of a religious folk song, proceeding from the "inner shrine of religion, creating an atmosphere from which all worldly influences disappear, abstract, impersonal, and not the creation of an individual composer or his coloring through personal feeling and artistic impulse." An accomplished chanter and drill master himself, Gregory drew students from all parts of the continent, schooled them for nine years, and then sent them forth as masters of plainsong to Gaul, Britain, and Germany.

Gregorian tone or plainsong is just what the name indicates, the reciting of one note to each syllable, the rhythm, accent and movement being that of the text. It was unaccompanied and largely antiphonal. Later on, this plainsong encouraged floridity, several notes or many notes sung to one syllable, a decorative style reserved for the Ordinary of the Mass, and intoned by singers of luxurious tastes, vocal gymnasts, solo artists with long hair and wearing soft silken tunics.

These chanted by trilling the tongue against the roof of the mouth, caroling on vowel sounds as in *Alleluia, Amen* and *saecula saeculorum*, using tones to heighten the ground mood of words; in the language of Augustine: "He who jubilates does not utter any words, but a joyous sound without words; for it is the spirit lost in joy, expressing it with all its powers, but not arriving at a definition of its sense." Mystery of the unseen Presence!

Thus and thus only did the art of music break the shackles of words, with monks playing with notes as children play with toys, turning tunes upside down, inside out, over into monograms and puzzles, a jargon of *melismas*. But without these centuries of holidays there could have been no Palestrina, Bach or William Byrd. Music thus entered upon a career of its own, building its own alphabet, grammar, rhetoric, literature through recitative, plainchant, ornate cadences and melodies, and the polyphony of the fifteenth and sixteenth centuries.

A second school, that of polyphony or the science of weaving many voice parts together, reached its culmination in Palestrina and at a period when the Catholic Church was subject to adverse criticism both from within and without, with the reform movements in Prague, Zurich, Wittenberg and Geneva getting under way. Consummate of skill, noble of character, of rapt and mystical piety, was this saviour of tonal art from mechanical and mathematical excesses: Giovanni Pierluigi da Palestrina (1525–1594) master of choral song in his home town, Palestrina, and later at Santa Maria Maggiore, St. John Lateran, and St. Peter's, Rome. His was cathedral singing, which often began with a filament of tone as delicate as spider's webbing, joined by tauter and looser threads of tone, welling up into gossamer sheen but never into coarse *fortissimos* (stentorian singing is a product of the nineteenth century), choir answering choir, and closing with velvety, sustained cadences. Without orchestra or organ, Palestrina swept primary and secondary colors into his compositions, creating beauty of tone and sonorous ensemble through "his manner of grouping notes, his alternation of lower with higher voices, his resolution of clouded polyphony into sun bursts of open chords, his subtle transformation of dissonances into gleaming concord, and his skilful blending of vocal registers for startling contrasts of light and shade." [8] There is no parallel in modern choral writing with his impersonalized, mystical, interpretative setting of the Mass. Palestrina remains the cornerstone of church choral music.

This choral style merits mastery today: floating tone, not noisy; beautiful, not ravishing; impersonal, not carnal. The simpler anthems of this school, *Adoremus te, O bone Jesu, Jesu, dulcis memoria,* will attract more and better singers, for such art demands laboratory exactitude, sensitivity of ear, tone color variation, balance of parts and impeccable team work. Its habit is to extend meanings not by more words, but through expressive use of tones, nevertheless moving straight through to the end in the shortest possible time, and should therefore be welcomed to stream-lined morning services. It tolerates no vain repetition of words—contrast a recent choral number, covering eight pages, one hundred measures, three hundred chords, whose choral chest expands to utter four words only: "Long life and glory, glory and long life" thirty-three consecutive times!

Our next concern is with three theologians and spiritual empire builders, who as hymn writers, organizers of choirs, and founders of church music schools, fostered music as a democratic, profitable plan of life.

The astonishment that one experiences in the opera *Sieg-*

---

[8] Edward Dickinson: *Music in the History of the Western Church.*

*fried* comes on hearing Brünnehilde, waked from her sleep by a magic kiss, SING! a woman's voice, after ninety minutes of man's somber soloing and choral intoning. The Reformation was ushered in by such a burst of soprano tone, women singing after being muted through three thousand years. This mistress of melody has been an accredited church singer during the past four hundred years only.

Martin Luther, at Wittenberg, 1529 ,wrote his first German hymn and tune, "Ein Feste Burg ist unser Gott," which started a flood of lyrics and tunes, resounding early and late, amid affairs of business, in every street and market place, bringing to men's lives "space for rejoicing and adoration." While dissolving cathedral choirs as such, he organized peregrinating units to travel from town to town on festival days, inspiring plain folks to sing unison, while the singers themselves filled in the other parts.

Luther wrote songs for his people that God might speak directly to them through his Word, and that they might directly answer him in their songs. Our habit today is largely not to answer Him, but rather to sing one to another a memorandum of events in our own lives, how we feel, how we fail, with largeness in the pronoun I. This is empirical song, subjective, mirroring our own inner states. One may participate in so-called evangelistic singing through a year of Sundays, and never address God directly, intimately. Reformation song was Godward, praise and prayer to the Rock, the Fortress, the Deliverer, Lord Sabbaoth is His name!

The German Reformation championed another movement which started in the thirteenth century, the sound of outdoor singing, of pilgrims on the march, of troubadours, minnesingers, and mastersingers, noteworthy in permitting plain folk to vie with the hierarchy in the writing and singing of folk songs, madrigals, and dramatic *lieder,* much of it sacred, some good, some bad; nevertheless a striking expression of democracy and of faith and works.

Ever and anon music becomes over heavy, dried up to its very center, self-righteous in its own finesse. One dare not always be a "rider of principles." Paraphrasing Jeremiah Reeves: "The music of the people is not an alien thing, apart from them; it is of course expressed at first by a few elect spokesmen, but after all it is of, and for, the many. It cannot be deemed estranged and aloof. If to be musicianly is to be cabined, cribbed, apart from the common mind and heart of the age, the folk song and hymn are not music and litera-ture. But literature is not thus penned up away from the people. It springs forth from the general consciousness as a spring of water issues from the hillside. And it is assigned to its place by the social mind." [9]

Luther fits into this picture of people's song because of his philology which came from the mouths of the common peo-ple, whereas his tunes, many of them, were arrangements from popular home, love, and patriotic songs. For example, in a secular song book, edited after Luther's day by Hans Leo Hassler, entitled *A Pleasure Garden of New German Songs, Balleti, Galliards, and Intrades,* is to be found a love song in five stanzas, in acrostic form, the initial letters spelling MARIA; the song being "My peace of mind is shattered by the charms of a tender maiden." By changing the rhythm from 6/8 into 4/4, enriching the harmonies and slowing down the pace, evolves the *Passion Chorale* for "O sacred Head, now wounded."

Luther's church song powerfully aided the new faith to maintain itself in the midst of conflict, and it did set up the democratic traditions of German art as over against the aristocratic trends in Italy and France.

The next master of musical practice lived at Geneva, John Calvin, who continues to be villified for banishing corporate worship, symbolism, art windows, vestments, instruments,

---

[9] Jeremiah Bascom Reeves: *The Hymn in History and Literature.*

and all singing except unison. He did, however, summon to his Auditoire the most distinguished French musicians and poets of his day, among them, Louis Bourgeois, who came from Paris and was granted the rights of citizenship "in consideration of his being a respectable gentleman and willing to teach children." Tunes from the Genevan Psalter of 1552 and 1562 are rapidly coming into use in this country: *Old Hundredth* (with alternating long and short notes), *Old 124th* or *Toulon, Donne Secours, L'Omnipotent,* and *Old 38th* and *42d.* These and chorales from Germany, as also staunch Anglican and American tunes should be first in the love of children, for anything can be stamped upon their open and receptive minds. The blighting of children's musical taste and frustration of their worship experience in the name of religion, must stop!—through stunt piano playing, secular tunes and rhythms led by a cheer leader, the subject matter being largely sin and eschatology.

Of all the monuments reared by Calvin, none is more enduring than his Genevan *Psalter* and the exalted melodies taken therefrom for the enrichment of children's art life and their Christian nurture. As a romanticist he declared: "Has not the Creator given beauty to gold, to silver, to ivory, to marble? Has he not given to us many things which we hold in esteem although they are not necessary to us? Let us refuse to accept the inhumane philosophy which, refusing to concede to man any use of the good creatures of God except on the grounds of necessity, having robbed him of all sentiment, it has turned him into a log of wood."

The final empire builder through song lived and worked at Herrnhut, near Dresden in Germany, Count von Zinzendorf, famous for his writing and use of hymns during the first half of the eighteenth century. His first hymnal, compiled and issued in 1725, *Sammlung geistlicher und lieblicher Lieder,* had a curious mixture of tunes: chorales of the Moravians themselves, a few popular melodies, a large inclusion of old Roman Catholic music and the best from the churches of the Reformation period.

His hymns and tunes, particularly with children, became material for instruction, precise, factual, comprehensive, and inspirational. His teaching use of hymns is unparalleled in the history of religious education, while his choir system surpasses the multiple choir system of today. His eleven choirs were:

> Choir of Infants in Arms
> Choir of Little Children
> Choir of Boys
> Choir of Girls
> Choir of Older Boys
> Choir of Older Girls
> Choir of Young Men
> Choir of Young Women
> Choir of Married People
> Choir of Widows
> Choir of Widowers [10]

Mother church is alive with singers today; a cross section of human life enters its doors to sing in graded choral units, with the norm of the average parish three in number, an adult mixed chorus, a youth choir and a junior choir of girls. If perchance a boy choir of unchanged voices is added, be it known to the unsuspecting that the most mischievous are the top-notch singers, for they have the spirit of adventure, the initiative, the imagination, the bravado to take punishment without flinching, of high notes, unhesitating attack, long phrases, and sustained climax.

During the acts of worship, what feelings are to be manifested in the choir loft, what moods of expression voiced

---

[10] Henry H. Meyer: *Child Nature and Nurture according to Zinzendorf.*

for the people? How many church musicians best serve the congregation?

1. Through singing *with* the congregation on hymns, chants, and responses, and through leading in responsive readings and attitudes of prayer. The congregation is not an unmitigated nuisance because of imperfect singing, but a willing, pliable body of worshipers to be led by strong social integration, a singing fellowship, and a missionary heart on the part of choristers. The choirs thus supply tonal, rhythmical, intellectual and spiritual guidance.

2. That of singing *for* the congregation. Here the people, unable to join in the higher art forms of anthem, chorale, and short motet, sing silently, while choristers audibly voice prayer and praise, yearnings and ecstasies. For this vicarious act, singers should take the vows of chastity, humility and dedication, for only those of clean hands and pure hearts may rightly lift to the throne of grace the petitions and thanksgivings of a worshiping people.

3. That of singing *to* the congregation, the choir rendering a personal service as comforter and exhorter to each and every layman. Thus music is no longer a profession but a principle, with the singer an evangelist, with discerning instinct and sustained fervor, imparting his faith to others.

Choirs should emulate the masters of tone who knew God and served him. Handel protested to an Anglican bishop: "I have read my Bible: I shall choose for myself," and he did: arranged the text for his immortal Messiah in three major sections, the Incarnation, the Passion and Redemption, and the Kingdom of God in all the world. While writing his Hallelujah Chorus he exclaimed: "I did think I did see all heaven before me and the great God himself."

Haydn's gratitude was thus voiced: "Almighty God to whom I render thanks for all his unnumbered mercies, gave me such facility in music that by the time I was six years old,

I stood up like a man, and sang masses in the church choir."

Beethoven succinctly said: "God looks into my heart. He searches it and knows that love for man and feelings of benevolence have their abode there."

Concerning Cesar Franck, an authority writes: "He stands out from his contemporaries as one of another age. They are scoffers, he was a believer; they vaunt themselves, he worked in silence; they seek glory, he let it seek him; they shrink from nothing, concession, compromise, meanness; he performed his mission faithfully and, without counting the cost, left us the noblest example of uprightness."

John Sebastian Bach's monumental music was dual in motivation: "The sole end and aim of thorough-bass, like that of all music, should be nothing else than the glory of God and pleasant recreation." He was a staunch Lutheran, who worked in quasi-Catholic Leipzig, where the Latin language and the framework of the Mass were not altogether banished. His chiefest choral works are the *Mass in B minor* and the *Passion Music according to St. Matthew*. Through them he profoundly declares the salvation of the world through the death of Christ on the Cross. Even in the Mass he does not surrender his private religious consciousness, his personality, his inner world of experience. Bach fervently followed his bent of "pleasant recreation." With his piety unconsciously coloring all, he went to work at his small organ. He transcended it. He made musical technique his spiritual medium. Master of form and of improvisation, his was absolute music, undisturbed by politics and doctrinal strife, by theology and dogma, for Lutheran hymns were singularly free from proof texts and ecclesiastical fiats. Bach was a free man even in the midst of the stiff rationalism of the eighteenth century; he went his way, happy in his own new empire of music. Gesner, rector of St. Thomas church in Bach's time, describes him: "Could you only see him presiding over thirty or forty performers all at once, recalling this one with a nod, that by a stamp of the foot, another with a warning finger, keeping time and tune! Great admirer as I am of antiquity, yet I am of the opinion that my Bach unites within himself many Orpheuses and twenty Arions!"

The Catholic and the German Evangelical systems of church music and their masters stand supreme. The English and American systems are of less moment. Nowhere has music been a keener two-edged sword, a fiercer fighting weapon, than in England during the fifteenth, sixteenth, and seventeenth centuries. Controversies were political first, religious second, the government for or against the Papacy. Gregorian chant was arrayed against folksong styles; polyphonic choral literature versus a new style of composition, the anthem; Psalmody striking at the heart of original hymns; organ construction pitted against its destruction. The Kingdom's *Schola Cantorum* was the Chapel Royal, the religious establishment of the sovereigns, whether at Greenwich, Whitehall, St. James Palace, or Windsor Castle; and here England's most noted musicians served, first as choir boys, then as organists, and masters of choirs: during the Tudor period, Thomas Tallis and William Byrd, and later John Blow, Henry Purcell, William Croft, Jeremiah Clark, and Orlando Gibbons. Many of these gentlemen, receiving appointments to St. Paul's, Westminster Abbey, and Ely, Hereford, Worcester cathedrals, founded choir schools therein. Their music covered the Palestrina style, the motet, the harmonized chant, the solo and verse and full anthem, with and without accompaniment; imbibing elegance from the Elizabethan period and not a little of its literary grace and charm, absorbing stable lines and light and shade from Romanesque and Gothic cathedrals, and brilliance and gay atmosphere from European opera.

This kaleidoscopic character of England's church music assured variety if not spirituality for her hours of ceremony.

T. F. Kinloch observes that "in Elizabethan times the Anglican did not hesitate to put his hat on the communion table; in Jacobean times he walked about St. Paul's while divine service was going on, to interview client or engage a servant; in the 18th century the squire sat in his curtained pew and no man knew how he comported himself; during the Oxford movement he conducted himself in more reverent fashion." [11]

The Oxford movement and the Victorian era of British music proved the most prolific period for the writing of tunes and anthems, characterized by Dr. Davison as "the assembling merely of an aggregation of notes arranged with words; serving to fill out a period of service, however a deplorably pale sacrifice." [12] Much of it was barren and routined in manufacture, diffuse and long-drawn-out to care for solos, organ intermezzos, and full chorus. On the other hand, the galaxy of composers were God-fearing men, devoted to the church, and drill masters of the most exacting sort. Choir boys in their early days, they grew up within the parish, were educated at Oxford or Cambridge, and went on to composing and to rearing choirs of extraordinary skill. Their names are household words to both the English and American church singer: George Elvey, George Martin, Frederick Ouseley, Arthur Sullivan, John Stainer, John Goss, Berthold Tours and Charles Villers Stanford; and the tune writers, Joseph Barnby and John Bacchus Dykes. England's twentieth-century church music will be briefly treated under American music.

## IV. RELIGIOUS MUSIC IN AMERICA

The earth was without form and void; and darkness was upon the face of the deep. And the spirit of God moved upon the face of the waters. And God said: Let there be light, and there was light.

---

[11] T. F. Kinloch: *An Historical Account of the Church Hymnary.*
[12] Archibald Davison: *Protestant Church Music in America.*

Four hundred and fifty years of American music, three hundred of them in the church music zone: and we find the Western world much in the chaos of primeval days. Discerning music students, masters of composition, professors of musicology, artists of distinction, conductors of symphony orchestras, spokesmen for music schools, and music critics have assigned to church music the lowest rung on the ladder. Denominational commissions on music have come and gone; art guilds spring into life, gasp for breath through a few short years, and expire. There is no sounding board that radiates purposes and principles, organization and administration, for a master-music plan at the heart of every parish.

American history opens with song, the *Salve Regina* as intoned by Columbus and his crew as they landed on San Salvador. The first book printed in America was a collection of songs, the *Bay Psalm Book*, on the Harvard College Press, 1640. Three youthful clergymen, headed by Rev. John Tufts of Roxbury, started a reform in 1719 of singing by note (the new way) as opposed to singing from memory or by rote (the old way). Sermons were preached, literature circulated, hymnals with tunes published. In 1770 the redoubtable Williams Billings, of Charlestown, Mass., invented fuguing tunes and organized singing schools. Illiterate, deformed, eccentric, with never a music lesson in his life, he determinedly set all New England singing. Lowell Mason, father of American church song, with his control extending from the Atlantic seaboard to the Western Reserve, and beyond the Mississippi, introduced music into the public schools, organized singing schools, musical institutes, conventions, and invariably identified himself with all churches and church schools within his reach.

Space will not permit reviewing the solo quartet as America's premier Levites in the temple during the decades from

1870 to 1900, nor the tuneful anthem literature of Dudley Buck, Harry Rowe Shelley, Will C. Macfarlane, James H. Rogers, Horatio Parker, and F. Flaxington Harker, of this same period and overlapping into the twentieth century. The present century among composite and democratic nations will not witness any concerted plan of action nor uniform type of church music. It is this very eclectic way of life among English and American composers which is lifting their church choral literature to rank with Catholic, German Evangelical and Russian styles. Whether Gregorian, polyphonic, harmonic, chantlike or in anthem form, the following Britishers and Canadians have adorned cathedral, chapel and nonliturgic edifices with beauty, resonance, and mystery: Gustav Holst, Ralph Vaughan Williams, John Ireland, Martin and Geoffrey Shaw, Basil Harwood, Healey Willan, and Alexander Whitehead.

The problem is not one of creation today, but of administration. Composers are as free, as was Bach, to say what they will through patterns of notes. Conscious of orchestral color, of the *a cappella* choir regime, of racial reservoirs of feeling, American tone-poets are gravitating toward the church to help make her unconquerable through song: Canon Douglas, Everett Titcomb, F. Meluis Christiansen, T. Tertius Noble, Clarence Dickinson, Mrs. H. H. A. Beach, David Mc K. Williams, and Leo Sowerby. More antiphonal forms are in the making, descant waves its white plume of notes, the "music makers" are here, and as "dreamers of dreams," and with a "new song's measure," they are the "movers and shakers" of a spiritual world forever.

## V. Universal Song

From this brief survey of sacred tonal art, may we turn to the practical side of building an empire of church song:

Everyone suddenly burst out singing,
And I was filled with such delight
As prisoned birds must find in freedom,
Winging wildly across the white
Orchards and dark green fields,
On, on, out of sight!
Everyone's voice was suddenly lifted;
And beauty came like the setting sun.[13]

Moral and spiritual victory through singing hearts may be achieved by following the rules of Universal Song:

1. For every hour of listening in, there shall be an hour of creating one's own music. Laboratory singing should be stepped up.

2. Those who have never sung will launch into singing: all who have become silent, will again break into song; any who have habitually sung unison, will venture into part singing.

3. All song will be a four-fold blessing: granting stronger and longer life; evoking more chastened emotions; arousing friendlier feelings; deepening spiritual experiences.

4. All clergymen will shepherd a Song Crusade.

5. All chairmen of public assemblies will honor song by lifting it to high place, and not permit it to become a door mat on which the unthinking wipe their feet.

6. People of refinement and lovers of art will not be driven from their pews by doggerel and hack verses, trivial tunes, pretentious directing and playing, as if God were only a friendly sort of host.

7. The fact that folks love to sing will be discounted. They do not ordinarily; everything is set against them:

a. Human beings talk easily and freely, not so when singing; for lungs must be expanded beyond their norm, necessitating sustained muscular effort.

---

[13] Poem by Siegfried Sassoon.

b. The larynx is a double-reed mouthpiece, two membranes, swinging toward and away from each other, letting out successive puffs of air per second for tone production. These vocal chords become strained and fatigued, as also the throat; one should not sing WITH it, but THROUGH it.

c. Resonance is ordinarily lacking, tones being dark rather than white. Forward placement calls for humming and vocalizing against the bridge of the nose and back of the eyes.

d. Diction necessitates determined and meticulous articulation via jaw, tongue, lips, palate, and cheek bones, particularly when vowels, the singing center of words, are hedged in by consonants, as in

> "The rockets' red glare,
> The bombs bursting in air."

This is not too high for an American audience, but too much of an impenetrable jungle of r's and b's.

8. Organists and leaders of song will be idealists—will lift their congregations through interpretative, colorful singing, and not flatten them out. Singing monotony is an arch sin. No two hymns, no two anthems, are exactly alike. A love for adventure, for new continents to be explored, will find realization through changes of pace and power, through building of climaxes by raising keys stanza by stanza, through descant and faux bourdon, and by climactic endings as in the *Netherland's Folk Song* coda, and in the *Austrian Hymn* which in Europe is repeated through the last four measures *maestoso, fortissimo,* epochal. Comments on church music will be factual, terse, dramatic, while Scripture verses between stanzas will make the singing antiphonal besides clarifying thought content.

9. Certain choral units, ensconced in chancel or choir gallery, will move to the pews and sing in the midst of the people, thus transforming feeble song into confident outpouring of

tone. There is definite isolation for any and all laymen who "sing out." They are immediately set apart as lusty, ambitious creatures, solo voices in the midst of intermittent mumblings.

10. The format of the hymnal will be that of the words printed within the music staff, and not at the foot of the page, necessitating a mental track meet between music "up there" and words "down here." There will be enough hymn books, wisely distributed, and their upkeep will be assured—no torn and missing pages, with monograms and cartoons sprinkled through, an altogether unlovely and derelict book.

Lighting, direct and indirect, will be stepped up in seventy-five per cent of auditoriums and sanctuaries, so that would-be singers may not be compelled to guess at text and tune, but may see the printed page in white light. Beatific dim illumination is provocative of mystery, but not of forthright singing.

11. Mother Church will no longer continue its closed-door policy, open many of them only one hour per week, sixty out of 10,080 minutes; tax free, equipped with noble organs, comfortable seats, resonant auditoriums, comfort and warmth and asylum. The Sabbath was made for man, not man for the Sabbath, i.e., not one service but three and four a Sunday as in the Fourth Presbyterian, Chicago, the First Congregational, Los Angeles, Foundry Methodist in Washington, D. C. and Catholic churches; inviting parishioners to worship when they are free to come; a pre-snow train service as in Emmanuel Church, Boston; a golfers' special at Southern Pines, an early morning service for early risers and for cooks of the American Sunday dinner, a vesper service for those who would not miss Jack Benny, the Quiz Kids, Charlie McCarthy, and Fred Allen, and an evening service for those intent on evangelistic meetings. Reform we will, not by counting attendance at one service, but glorying in three or four, timed for all who seek the kingdom of God.

12. Not one choir in the 100,000 Protestant churches dare go the way of non-essentials, disbanded for the duration. If Mother Church is not taking care of her children and youth, who is? Father is in the armed forces, mother in war industry, or in the Red Cross, or in Bundles for Britain, with no one at home to guide distraught and venturing young America. Juvenile crime is doubled over normal times. Furthermore, choir festivals should continue to bring all faiths together, for there is unity of race, creed and color through music. Rationing of travel is no explanation for the discontinuance of these events. Defeatism in the spiritual world is. Downtown churches are at the very center of urban life, and within easy walking distance of multitudes who seek the quiet, the strength, the joy, that comes through universal song.

The massing of all faiths is not something to be dreamed about; it is here. Jews, Catholics, Protestants, Public Schools, Civic Organizations, Women's Clubs are touching singing elbows; we live together, we are neighbors one of another; why not sing together?

13. The minister of music will be a new creature. He will have a professional view of his ministry, growing all the time and not caught in a stalemate, contacting idealists and master craftsmen in his field. He will moreover be a vocational minister, view his calling as sacred, a priesthood, guiding his singers into the eternal mysteries. Such a minister of music will widen his studies and interests to include liturgics, hymnology, the Bible, religious education, church history, poetry and literature, social behavior, and business management (Plate XXIII). In studying the trends of American life he will have discovered that our people are wearily abandoning principle for what-do-we-care philosophy, "which holds that any crookedness short of downright criminality is all right if it is clever and if it produces results. This attitude or resignation is the result of constant attacks on the morals of the country, first on one front, then on another."

One popular song has caused the name of God to be sung by almost all of the 130,000,000 Americans: "Praise the Lord and pass the ammunition." Rev. Paul Martin adds: "How strange it is that so many of those who take this sacred name on their lips know nothing of his wondrous person and works. Here is what they are actually doing: they are passing the Lord and praising the ammunition. For, does not America boast of its productive capacity, and that our planes, tanks, and ammunition will eventually blow the enemy right out of the war?" [14]

A final word should be said concerning the interrelation of the arts, particularly music and speech, as strikingly integrated in a *Lincoln Portrait,* for Orchestra and Narrator, by Aaron Copeland, and given its recent premières both in Boston and New York by Will Geer and the Boston Symphony Orchestra. It is a portrait of Lincoln with the sitter himself speaking; portraying the mysterious sense of fatality that surrounded Lincoln, and his gentleness and simplicity of spirit; also the background of the times in which he lived; and finally a simple but impressive frame about the words of Lincoln himself. If symphonic tone and speech can combine in such epochal fashion to portray history and biography, why should not the expression of religion expand its media of introits, choral apostrophes, congregational antiphons, organ fantasias, rhetorical speech, into one epochal art form? Here perchance is the Kingdom and the Power and the Glory!

During the reading of this Portrait, bear in mind that the orchestra is playing continuously, coloring every word, sentiment, lineament of Lincoln.

"Fellow citizens, we cannot escape history."
That is what he said,
That is what Abraham Lincoln said:

---

[14] *Congressional Record,* Jan. 26, 1943. A sermon by Paul Martin.

PLATE XXIII (A)

YOUTH CHOIRS OF THE SECOND PRESBYTERIAN CHURCH, BLOOMINGTON, ILLINOIS

PLATE XXIII (B)

CHORAL ARTS SINGERS, BOSTON UNIVERSITY

Dr. H. Augustine Smith, Founder and Director

PLATE XXIV (A)

SCENE IN AN AIR-RAID SHELTER

From Dr. Eastman's play, "Eternal Life"

PLATE XXIV (B)

SCENE FROM "PAGEANT OF WORSHIP" WRITTEN BY DR. EASTMAN'S STUDENTS

First Congregational Church, Los Angeles

"Fellow citizens, we cannot escape history.
"We of this Congress and this administration will be remembered
  in spite of ourselves. No personal significance or insignificance
  can spare one or another of us.
"The fiery trial through which we pass will light us down,
  in honor or dishonor, to the latest generation.
  We—even here—hold the power and bear the responsibility."

He was born in Kentucky, raised in Indiana, and lived in Illi-
  nois.
This is what he said:
This is what Abe Lincoln said:
"The dogmas of the quiet past are inadequate to the stormy
  present.
The occasion is piled high with difficulty,
and we must rise with the occasion.
As our cause is new, so we must think anew and act anew.
We must disenthrall ourselves, and then we shall save our
  country."

When standing erect he was six feet four inches tall.
And this is what he said: he said:
"It is the eternal struggle between two principles—
right and wrong throughout the world. . . .
It is the same spirit that says:
'You toil and work and earn bread and I'll eat it.'
No matter in what shape it comes,
whether from the mouth of a king who seeks
to bestride the people is his own nation and live
by the fruit of their labor, or from one race of men
as an apology for enslaving another race,
it is the same tyrannical principle."
Lincoln was a quiet man.

Abe Lincoln was a quiet and a melancholy man.
But when he spoke of democracy,
This is what he said: he said:
"As I would not be a slave, so I would not be a master.
This expresses my idea of democracy.
Whatever differs from this, to the extent of the difference,
is no democracy."

Abraham Lincoln, sixteenth President of these United States,

is everlasting in the memory of his countrymen,
for on the battleground at Gettysburg, this is what he said:
This is what Abe Lincoln said:
"That from these honored dead we take increased devotion
to that cause for which they gave the last full
measure of devotion:
that we here highly resolve that these dead
shall not have died in vain; that this nation, under God,
shall have a new birth of freedom;
and that the government of the people, by the people,
for the people, shall not perish from the earth." [15]

# *Bibliography*

Willard Learoyd Sperry: *Reality in Worship*. The Macmillan
    Company, 1925
    Historical, philosophical and liturgical treatment of worship,
    with emphasis on the tripartite patterns of thesis, antithesis,
    and synthesis, and objective worship in the historic liturgies
    as over against subjective worship in the free churches.

Clarence Seidenspinner: *Form and Freedom in Worship*. Willett,
    Clark and Company, 1941
    Liturgic form and materials, architecture, and the church year
    of earlier centuries not adapted to the worship of today.
    Craftsmen with revised language, new emphasis, new expan-
    sions, for contemporaneous American life. The genius of music
    in worship.

A. Z. Idelsohn: *Jewish Music—in Its Historical Development*.
    Henry Holt and Company, 1929
    The song of the synagogue from earliest times through 3500
    years as noted in Oriental and European Jewish communities.
    The musical modes of song and prayer, the rhythmical modes
    and decorative styles of Oriental centers, with musical illus-
    trations largely in modern notation.

---

[15] *Boston Symphony Orchestra program,* April 9, 1943, material assembled
by Aaron Copland. Printed with the permission of the copyright owners,
Boosey and Hawkes, Inc., 43 West 23rd St., New York City.

Matthew Britt: *The Hymns of the Breviary and Missal*. Benziger
   Brothers, 1922
   Complete Latin texts of 173 Catholic Hymns, with vivid and
   literal prose translations followed by translations into lyric
   verse by seventy-three Protestant and Catholic versifers. The
   nature of Catholic worship and its delineation through hymns.

Edward Dickinson: *Music in the History of the Western Church*.
   Charles Scribner's Sons, 1902
   Reverent, scholarly, eclectic survey of church music from primi-
   tive times, with three major emphases: (1) that of the Catholic
   Liturgy, Ritual Chant, Medieval choral music, and Modern
   Mass; (2) that of Lutheran Hymnody, German cantata and
   passion, and John Sebastian Bach; (3) the Music System of
   the Church of England.

Winfred Douglas: *Church Music in History and Practice*. Charles
   Scribner's Sons, 1937
   Foundation principles of church music. Music of the Eucharist,
   past and present, and of the Daily Offices. The evolution of
   hymnody. Extended lists of phonographic records by world
   famous choirs, covering every phase of liturgical choral practice.

Archibald Thompson Davison: *Protestant Church Music in
   America*. E. C. Schirmer Music Co., 1933
   A thought-provoking book, with the iconoclast breaking down
   pet theories and current practices, and then building a noble
   edifice of choral song. Discriminating in its treatment of sacred,
   religious, and secular song. Authoritative handling of absolute
   music. Copious illustrations.

William James Henderson: *Early History of Singing*. Longmans,
   Green and Company, 1921
   Unusual source material concerning early chanters, the *Schola
   Cantorum,* the Troubadours, and the medieval vocal teachers.
   Early ideals concerning singing. Timely and interesting.

T. F. Kinloch: *An Historical Account of the Church Hymnary*
   (Revised). W. Heffer and Sons, Ltd., Cambridge, England,
   1928
   Worth its weight in gold. Ninety pages of historical and critical

summaries of hymns, with corrected data, freshening observations, astute relationships to human life—the desperate fight which hymns have made to win favor.

Myles Birket Foster: *Anthems and Anthem Composers*. Novello and Company, Ltd., 1901
The development of the anthem from the Reformation to the end of the nineteenth century, with complete listings of anthems and names and lives of composers through four hundred years. Discerning study of the great and near-great in English music.

George Grove: *Grove's Dictionary of Music and Musicians*. The Macmillan Company, 1935 (Third Edition, ed. by Henry Cope Colles)
The recognized standard work of reference in the English language on music, with the third edition entirely revised and reset and brought up to date.

Isabel Florence Hapgood: *Service Book of the Holy-Orthodox-Catholic-Apostolic Church*. Association Press, 1922
A compilation, translation, and arrangement of the All-night vigil service, the divine liturgy of St. John Chrysostom and of St. Basil the Great (the Mass of the Greek and Russian churches), and other liturgic forms.

# IV

## THE DRAMATIST AND THE MINISTER

*By* FRED EASTMAN

DR. FRED EASTMAN came through the pastorate and literary work to his present position as Professor of Biography, Literature and Drama, in the faculty of the Chicago Theological Seminary. He has occupied this chair since 1926, and in that time has become known nationally in the field of religious drama. His literary output has been varied and extensive. He is the author of a large number of religious dramas, several books and many magazine contributions. Among the better known of his books are "Fear God in Your Own Village" (1918), "Drama in the Church" (1933), "Books That Have Shaped the World" (1937), a five-volume series "Men of Power" (1938–1940). Among his play-pageants may be listed "America's Unfinished Battles," "The Triumph of the Undefeated," "America on Trial"; and of his plays the following—"Bread," "The Tinker," "The Great Choice," "Our Lean Years" and "The Examination."

# IV

## THE DRAMATIST AND THE MINISTER

WHAT CAN THE MINISTER LEARN from the dramatist? More specifically, what can the minister learn from the dramatist that will make preaching and the conduct of a service of worship more effective? To answer that question, at least in part, is the purpose of this discussion.

### I

Let us begin with a brief consideration of the relation of religion and drama. The salvation of the world is the goal of religion. But religion, to be effective, must be dramatized. It cannot be presented effectively in abstractions. The word "drama" means *deeds* or *acts*. To dramatize anything is to present it in action so that people may see it with their eyes, hear it with their ears, and carry the memory of it in their imaginations. God has dramatized his love for man in a thousand ways, but supremely in the life of Jesus—"The word became flesh and dwelt among us." That is still the world's greatest drama.

Jesus dramatized religion in his teaching as well as in his life. The stories of the Prodigal Son and the Good Samaritan are typical examples of the way in which he portrayed religion in action. Even the most ignorant could understand and appreciate a religious message so graphically told. Our greatest teachers have always dealt in deeds, related with imaginative power. They have made the truths of religion stand out so vividly that the wayfaring man, though a fool, could not miss their force. Today we need ministers who can do this for our stricken generation. We need men who not only have a vital gospel to preach but who know how to dramatize that gospel in their sermons, their church-schools and their communities. They must make that gospel live in the imaginations of Christians.

Is not this the point at which so many young ministers fail? They may have a gospel but they preach it in abstractions; their church schools limp along, earth-bound and wingless; and their community work is a round of committee meetings. They formulate fine programs but they set few hearts afire. Their own imaginations are still unkindled, their vocabularies frozen in the ice of academic lingo. As Halford Luccock says, speaking of their sermons, "The voice may be the voice of God, but the hand that writes the words is the hand of John Dewey."

How can we expect anything else, considering the one-sided nature of their preparation for the ministry? In college they specialized in science; in seminary they concentrated in distinctly theological fields. In both they cultivated their intellects and left their imaginations untutored. The result: at best, inarticulate scholars; at worst, dry and windy parsons.

Drama rightly used can make a positive contribution toward righting this one-sided development. It can kindle imaginations; it can purge and exalt emotions; it can translate ideas into action. The minister who wants to learn the secret will do well to study the work of the dramatist, for the minister himself should be something of an artist, and among all the artists he has most in common with the dramatist.

## II

Consider next what the dramatist and the minister have in common.

They have a deal of *history* in common. In the early years

of every civilization this planet has known, religion and drama, if not born of the same mother, have at least shared the same cradle. Take only one example, that of ancient Greece. Drama there began in the temple of Dionysus, god of fertility and vegetation. Out of the songs and dances in honor of the god came in time the great dramas of Aeschylus and Sophocles and Euripides. These dramas were essentially religious in character. They dealt with deep and timeless spiritual and social issues. They were presented in the most sacred spot in Athens and at the most sacred season of the year. During their production the poets who wrote the plays, the actors who played in them, and the choragi who directed them were counted as ministers of religion and their persons were held inviolable. The audiences for these dramas were enormous, numbering twenty thousand in a city whose total population was only thirty thousand. When the plays were being presented all business was adjourned and even the law courts were closed. But the jails were opened so that the prisoners might be led into the temple and receive the ethical and spiritual stimulus of the dramas.

But in Greece, as in other civilizations, as the drama grew in sophistication it lost its sense of spiritual mission and separated itself in time from religion. It began as a means of influencing the gods. Then, as the priesthood was established, it came to be a means of influencing the priests; and finally evolved into a means of influencing the people. The more it lost its orientation toward the gods and sought to appeal only for popularity among the people, the more it degenerated into a means of entertainment and escape from life rather than a means of interpretation of the struggles of life. So, as Dr. Harry Emerson Fosdick once said, the drama, which began as a child of the church, grew up to be its prodigal son.

But today we have a new group of dramatists who are taking their art quite seriously as a means of interpreting life and not simply escaping from it. Maxwell Anderson in his *Prelude to Poetry in the Theatre* [1] states their attitude:

. . . the stage is still a cathedral, but just now a journalistic one, dominated by those who wish to offer something immediate about our political, social or economic life. Like every other existing condition it gives the illusion of permanence, but it will change. An age of reason will be followed once more by an age of faith in things unseen. The cathedral will then house the mysteries again. . . . We shall not always be as we are—but what we are to become depends on what we dream and desire. The theatre more than any other art, has the power to weld and determine what the race dreams into what the race will become.

Many of our other able and serious dramatists—Eugene O'Neill, Philip Barry, Paul Green, Sidney Kingsley, S. N. Behrman, Robert Sherwood, Marc Connelly, and Thornton Wilder, to mention a few—are producing such effects with the best of their plays. The minister would be blind indeed who did not recognize his community of interest with these playwrights.

The minister has in common with a serious dramatist certain *aims*. Both aim to arouse and hold the interest of an audience. Both seek to interpret for that audience some phase of life in such a way that the audience has its mind stimulated, its emotions stirred, and its imagination stored with vital images. Each has other aims in addition to these, but these common aims are basic to both.

They have certain *media* in common. The media through which both work are speech, music, and lighting effects. No one will quarrel, of course, with the inclusion of speech, and few with the inclusion of music. Many ministers are still unaware that the lighting effects in their churches have any relation to their sermons or to the success of their worship

---

[1] The Preface to *Winterset*, Anderson House. Used by permission.

services, but their unawareness does not alter the fact. We shall deal with this later.

Both have a common *limitation in time*. The dramatist must achieve his aims with his audience in two hours or a little over. The minister is even more limited. If his church service runs over an hour and a quarter, the congregation gets restless, watches are pulled out, feet are shuffled, and other signs given to indicate that the effort to save souls has run into conflict with the law of diminishing returns.

Further, the dramatist and the minister have in common a dependence for their success upon their *effect* upon the audience. In either case if the audience goes out unmoved or only critical, the effort has been a failure no matter how much time and labor went into its preparation. On the other hand, if the audience goes away exalted in spirit, its imagination stimulated, and its will to action challenged, the effort is a success. The minister or the dramatist can then look forward to future congregations and audiences.

### III

Consider, now, what the dramatist and the minister have in *difference*. One has his audience in a theater, the other his congregation in a church. The *buildings* are radically different in architecture. The theater is so arranged that the entire attention of the audience is focused upon the stage and on a single group of players upon that stage.[2] The focus of attention of the congregation of a church is less concentrated. While the church pews face forward, the members who sit in them are much more aware of each other—and

---

[2] Fifty years ago many theaters had a diamond horseshoe of boxes so arranged that the attention of the audience would be focused upon the bespangled ladies who occupied those boxes. But these diamond horseshoes have vanished from the modern theater and are now only relics of the show-off days of the newly rich.

of any new hats which may have appeared—and their attention is sometimes upon the altar, sometimes upon the choir,
and for only a part of each service upon the minister.

There is a difference, too, in the *mood of the audience* in
theater and church. The mood of the theater audience is
for entertainment. That of the church audience is—presum-
ably—for worship. No matter how serious the dramatist's
purpose, he knows that he must keep his audience entertained. A Broadway producer once summed up in ten words
his advice to young playwrights: "Make 'em laugh, make
'em cry, and make 'em wait," he said. The minister has a
more charitable audience. He knows the people have not
come to be entertained. At best they have come for worship
and to seek fellowship with God and their fellows and the
perspectives of eternity upon their contemporary lives. At
worst they have come out of a sense of duty and with a mental
attitude of, "Well, here I am. I'm open to conviction, but I'd
like to see you convince me."

They differ, too, in this: the dramatist keeps himself out
of sight of the audience. Often the director and players wish
he would also keep himself out of their sight. But the minister, for better or worse, is almost constantly in the sight of
his congregation during the church service. And all through
the week he lives in a goldfish bowl. Thus the dramatist's
message is judged apart from his own visible personality and
conduct; whereas the minister's message is interpreted in
the light of his appearance, his mannerisms, and his daily
behavior.

Again they differ in the *human and mechanical aids* upon
which they depend for coöperation. The dramatist relies
upon professional producer and director, well-trained cast
and back-stage crew. The minister, on the other hand, must
depend (usually) upon amateur choir, church officers, and
student assistant (if any). The theater has a lighting system

designed to keep the attention of the audience upon the particular part of the stage where the action is taking place, while the rest of the theater is in darkness. The church, if typical of the average, has a lighting system that was installed in the horse and buggy days and was designed to illuminate a *room,* not to focus attention anywhere and certainly with no thought of lighting a service of worship. The theater's lights are manipulated by a skilled electrician who understands something of the relation of light to emotion. The church's lights are manipulated by a janitor who turns them all on at the beginning, all off at the close, and calls it a day.

But probably the most important of points of difference in the methods of the dramatist and the minister is the fact that the *minister is expected to preach,* and the *dramatist must not preach.* The minister is damned if he doesn't; the dramatist is damned if he does.

## IV

Having in mind these elements in common and in difference, let us turn to the question: how does a dramatist accomplish his purpose of arousing and holding interest while he interprets some phase of life in such a way that he sends his audience away with its imagination kindled, its intellect stimulated, and its emotions stirred? He does it first by *character portrayal.* Drama at its best is the art of creating characters so human that the audience recognizes its own kinship with them, of thrusting those characters into situations of intense conflict where they must make great and courageous choices, of revealing the spiritual forces which battle within them to a climax, and of resolving the struggle so honestly that the audience goes away feeling convinced that it has seen a slice of life truthfully interpreted.

To make our discussion graphic, let us examine a particular drama by a competent playwright and see how he goes about it. Let us choose John Galsworthy's play, "Loyalties," partly because it is a fine drama in its own right, partly because it deals with a theme which every minister must deal with frequently, and partly because Galsworthy himself has probably done more than any other dramatist to analyze his own methods.

The story of the play may be summarized briefly: A Jew named DeLevis, honest, well-to-do, and ambitious for membership in certain exclusive English clubs, is robbed of a thousand pounds while a guest at a week-end party in an English country home. Suspicion falls heavily upon another guest, Captain Ronald Dancy, an adventurous but reckless young man who has needed money to settle an unsavory affair with a woman of convenient morals and to keep the news of it from reaching his young wife whose faith in him is implicit. The other house-guests, all Gentiles and each loyal to his own social clique and club, soon line themselves up to stand by Dancy and against the Jew, DeLevis. They persuade Dancy that the only way to clear his name is to bring a civil action against DeLevis by charging him with defamation of character. Dancy with great reluctance yields to this persuasion and starts the law suit, engaging an attorney of the highest reputation, one Jacob Twisden. The case becomes the talk of the town in London.

Meanwhile DeLevis conducts his own investigation and digs up convincing evidence that Dancy is guilty of the theft. In spite of this evidence Dancy's Gentile friends, with one exception, all stand by him and bring every possible pressure to bear upon DeLevis to make him withdraw his evidence. They blackball him at the clubs to whose membership DeLevis aspired; they oust him from the organizations of which he is already a member, branding him as a cad and unfit for association with gentlemen. But DeLevis by this time no longer cares either for the return of the money, or for membership in the Gentile clubs. He has risen to a higher plane: he now wants justice maintained, the truth vindicated, and the honor of his race upheld.

The one Gentile who does not stand by Dancy is his own lawyer, Twisden. For when Twisden sees the evidence of Dancy's guilt, the old lawyer's loyalty to the high ideals of his profession constrain him to throw up the case. Dancy now faces prison. His young wife, distraught by his conviction, but loyal still, pleads with him to give himself up, promising to wait for him until the prison term is over and then to start life fresh in some new part of the world. But Dancy can't take it. He commits suicide as the police are hammering at his door.

So much for the outline of the play. Had the dramatist been interested only in the story, he could have told it in a few minutes. But even from this brief outline it is apparent that the story itself grows out of the characters and their conflicting loyalties. Galsworthy's prime interest is in those characters, bringing them to life in our imaginations so that we recognize them as flesh and blood persons like ourselves. The stage for him is a mirror of souls. Before the final curtain falls we know these characters better than many of us know our next-door neighbors.

We know these characters because Galsworthy knew them first and knew them down to the small, intimate factors of their lives. Concerning each character the dramatist asks himself such questions as these: How old is he? Where does he live? How does he earn his living? What is his annual income? Does he like his work? What fellowships does he have in it and what success? How does he spend his evenings? What kind of reading and music does he most enjoy? If he is married, to whom? Is it a happy marriage, and why? What elements of discord are in it? If he is single, why? What sort of mate does he want, if any? Is he Protestant, Catholic,

Jewish, Christian Science, or pagan? What things in life does he count most worth while? What sort of prayers does he make? What are his moral standards, individual and social?

With this background knowledge of the character's personality, the dramatist then comes to his major questions: What does the character want in this play? Who opposes him and why? What choice or choices does he have to make? By what standard of values does he make those choices? Only as a dramatist knows the answers to such questions can he expect to present his characters as living and recognizable human beings, and not simply puppets in a marionette show.

But knowing the characters is one thing, and being able to present them so that their inner qualities are revealed is another. How does Galsworthy, for example, accomplish character *revelation*?

He puts each character under a crisis in which such great pressures are brought to bear upon him that the character is broken open and we see his very soul. We see what each character wants. We see what choice he has to make. We see by what standard of values he makes his choices. We see what opposition he faces and what sustaining sources of power, if any, he possesses.

Look at the portrait which Galsworthy paints of each of the three central characters. There is DeLevis. What does he want? At first he wants only his money back. That is a superficial want. As the forces of race hatred and social prejudice are brought to bear upon him his deeper wants are revealed: the vindication of justice and the honor of his race. He has to choose whether or not he will stand by these things or overlook them in the interest of his own social advancement. Had his standard of value been only self-centered, he would have compromised, allowed Dancy to get away with the theft and claim for himself the social advance that was promised. But in the crisis a deeper standard of value comes to the surface—his own integrity and loyalty to his race. Making his choice by this standard, he meets with the opposition of practically every other character in the drama.

Then there is Jacob Twisden, the fine old lawyer. He wants justice, and believes at first that it is on the side of his client, Captain Dancy. When he is convinced of Dancy's guilt, he must choose between dropping the case and defending his client. The standard of value by which he makes his choice is his conviction that the integrity of the legal profession must be upheld. This brings him into opposition with Dancy's friends, but they are unable to change his decision.

Captain Ronald Dancy, when put under the pressure of the crisis which his theft has brought about, is revealed as a man who wants adventure and money to get himself out of a scrape. He must choose whether to plead guilty of theft or to plead not guilty and then try to escape before the evidence of conviction brings him to justice. His great weakness is that he has no standard of value beyond immediate self-interest by which to make the right choice. He begins by denying his guilt and seeking the protection of his friends in the army and in his social class. They stand by him loyally, and he has no opposition except from DeLevis. Ultimately, however, the truth comes out—the moral law has its innings, and he seeks escape in suicide.

When Galsworthy had created these characters and the dramatic crisis in which he was to reveal them, he had not yet made a drama. He had no more of a drama than a minister has a sermon when he has a good life situation and a few really recognizable human beings in it. The next thing for both is to work out the development of that situation in a series of episodes that show the characters in action in such a way that the interest of the audience is caught and held and heightened from minute to minute until the end is reached.

In this series of episodes by which the plot was developed Galsworthy made conscious and skillful use of the elements of dramatic interest which the ancient Greeks first discovered and utilized in the fierce competitions of their early dramatic contests. What are those elements of dramatic interest—in addition to characterization? Here are five of them: conflict, suspense, climax, emotion, and theme. Without these elements no amount of clever dialogue makes a play. With them carefully woven into a sustained pattern or plot, the interest of the audience is lifted in a crescendo.

*Conflict.* Next to characterization itself, the basic interest in most dramas, if not in all, roots in the clash of wills and personalities. If the central character were not put under the pressure of such a conflict the playwright could not break him open so that the audience could see what sort of person he is. It is sometimes said that drama was born among the Greeks when one character separated himself from the chorus, leaped upon the altar, and related a story of the sufferings of the god Dionysus. But real drama was not born until Aeschylus separated two characters from the chorus, lifted them to a stage and put them in conflict with each other. From that day on every poet who hoped to compete with Aeschylus in the dramatic contests knew he had to put his characters in a series of conflicts. By no lesser device could the attention of those 20,000 persons be held. And from that day to this all occidental drama makes use of this fundamental element of conflict. Throughout the two hours of Galsworthy's "Loyalties" there is hardly a moment when two or more of the characters on the stage are not in conflict.

*Suspense.* If the conflict is one-sided—one character so much stronger than the other that the audience is sure of the outcome—interest will lag. Therefore, every playwright who knows his craft sees to it that the persons in conflict are so nearly balanced that the issue is in doubt. By keeping that issue in doubt and the battle going from one round to the next, he keeps the audience from walking out.

*Climax*. The wise Greeks found that in addition to conflict and suspense they could increase the interest of the audience by arranging the various episodes of the major conflict in a sequence that built up to a climax. That was the highest point, where the struggle was fiercest, where the issue must be decided one way or another. In some of the ancient plays this climax came about half way through the play. The rest of it was devoted to more or less philosophical discussion of the effects of the struggle of the characters and upon similar struggles in the lives of the audience. But the audiences soon made it clear that they didn't care too much for such philosophical discussions; they preferred the dramas which ended shortly after the climax. Galsworthy ends "Loyalties" within two minutes of the moment when we are sure that Dancy's and DeLevis' struggle has reached its climax.

*Emotion*. Here is the element of human interest toward which all the others drive. A drama that does not reach the emotions fails, no matter how many fine ideas have been discussed in it. Percival Wilde rightly defines a drama as "an orderly representation of life, *arousing emotion in an audience*." Aristotle held that the highest function of drama was to produce a catharsis of the emotions of pity and fear by an exalted use of those passions. A typical member of the audience, before the drama starts, has in his heart a certain amount of self-pity and of fears for his own security and well-being. As the drama proceeds he becomes interested in some character upon the stage who is in trouble. Increasingly the member of the audience transfers his pity and his fear to that character upon the stage. This transference of pity and fear from oneself to someone else is an exalted use of those passions and has a cleansing effect—a catharsis of the emotions (Plate XXIV A).

Character, situation, story, and plot; conflict, suspense, climax, and emotion—there is yet one other great element in drama construction: theme. Here let Galsworthy speak for himself. In his essay, "Some Platitudes Concerning Drama," [3] he says:

A Drama must be shaped so as to have a spire of meaning. Every grouping of life and character has its inherent moral; and the business of the dramatist is so to pose the group as to bring that moral poignantly to the light of day. Such is the moral that exhales from plays like *Lear, Hamlet,* and *Macbeth.* But such is not the moral to be found in the great bulk of contemporary Drama. The moral of the average play is now, and probably has always been, the triumph at all costs of a supposed immediate ethical good over a supposed immediate ethical evil. . . .
. . . It was once said of Shakespeare that he had never done any good to any one, and never would. This, unfortunately, could not, in the sense in which the word "good" was then meant, be said of most modern dramatists. In truth, the good that Shakespeare did to humanity was of a remote, and, shall we say, eternal nature; something of the good that men get from having the sky and the sea to look at. And this partly because he was, in his greater plays at all events, free from the habit of drawing a distorted moral.

In "Loyalties" Galsworthy held rigidly to his conception of the dramatist's function concerning theme. The play has a *spire of meaning,* but nowhere is there any preaching of a moral. The theme—or spire of meaning—has to do with our clash of loyalties. We see each character in the play loyal to something—DeLevis to his race, Dancy to his own limited self-interest, Twisden to the legal profession, the club members to their clubs, the army men to their companions in arms. All this is human and right, so far as it goes. But yet it brings tragedy. Why? As one of the characters says, "Loyalties cut

---

[3] From *The Inn of Tranquillity.* Copyright, Charles Scribner's Sons. Used by permission.

up against each other sometimes . . . we all cut each other's throats with the best of intentions." That's as near as the theme is ever stated in words—but no thoughtful person can miss the deeper spire of meaning. These characters brought tragedy upon themselves because their minor loyalties had not been subordinated to one major loyalty that would include them all. They had given first-class loyalties to second-class values, and those lesser values had let them down. The dramatist does not say that; he simply presents a collection of very human persons acting that way and coming inevitably to grief.

When Galsworthy had finished his writing he next had to market his play—often as long and difficult a task as the composition itself. (Here the minister has a distinct advantage: he doesn't have to market his sermon. Suppose he did —but no, the thought is too terrifying! Let us return to the dramatist.) After Galsworthy had marketed his play, the producer engaged a director, cast, and crew. Thereupon the drama entered a new phase of its existence.

Skilled actors and technicians coöperated with one end in view: to squeeze every bit of emotional power out of that script and to send it across the footlights into the hearts of the audience. Scene builders provided the right background. Electricians assembled their lighting units and arranged them to accentuate the mood of each scene and to focus the attention of the audience upon the important characters at any given moment and to keep that attention from wandering anywhere else. All this and much more went on back of the curtain.

Meanwhile, other technicians had worked in front of the curtain. They saw to it that the seats were comfortable. They made sure that the air in the theater was fresh and at an even temperature. They made the entrance inviting. They exerted every effort to bring the play to the attention of the

public for which it was intended. If any of these artists and
technicians had neglected his job, the drama and all those
associated with it would have suffered. When their work was
done and the audience had gathered in the theater, the orchestra prepared it emotionally with music carefully selected
for that purpose. Then the lights in the theater dimmed out,
a moment of hushed expectancy followed, the curtain opened
and the characters began to unfold their tale of conflicting
loyalties.

In all of this Galsworthy was not unique. The same process
would have taken place had we chosen as an illustration
Thornton Wilder or Sidney Kingsley or Maxwell Anderson
or Eugene O'Neill or any other modern dramatist.

## V

What can the minister learn from this process? Is there
anything here that might help him in the preparation of his
sermons and in the conduct of a church service?

Let us deal first with the sermon. We shall trespass somewhat on the field of the professors of homiletics, but who
doesn't? That field has had more trespassers than a Kansas
wheat field has grasshoppers. Preaching is something like
hotel-keeping. "You don't have to know how to run a hotel,"
Jim Breslin used to say. "Just open one up and the customers
will tell you how to run it." Is there anyone within the reach
of these words who does not think he could give his minister
some points on preaching? Not a hand is raised. Therefore
let the homiletics professors remember that we are indulging
in a common human failing and be merciful.

George Tyrell predicted that in the last Judgment God
would not ask us what church we belonged to, but what
church we longed to create. Perhaps He will not ask the
minister about the sermons he preached, but about the
sermon he longed to preach. A seminary student once wrote

me of the kind of sermon he hoped some day to preach. "It is a sermon," he said, "that will tap for people their inner resources; that will cause to flow through their hearts a courage to make them heroic, a resolution to make them strong, a faith to bind them to the Eternal. In short, it is the sermon that will bring the power of God into the lives of men." What older minister does not hear in such words the echo of his prayers for his own preaching? Only God can answer the deep longing of such ministers, young and old. Our only attempt here is to suggest what human help may be found by applying to preaching some of the arts of the dramatist.

Here let two things be clearly understood. One is the difference between dramatic and theatrical preaching. Drama is the art; the theater is the institution that houses the art. The art at its best has dignity and depth and spiritual value. The building—the theater in which the drama is shown— should also have beauty and dignity. But all too often it is a show-house, gaudy, tinsled, ostentatious. For that reason in common practice when we describe something as "theatrical," we imply that it is affected, stilted, spectacular. Dramatic preaching, in the sense in which we are using it in this discussion, is never theatrical. It is always dignified, simple, natural. It is never theatrical—never showy, sensational, or shallow. Harry Emerson Fosdick is a good example of a dramatic preacher; Billy Sunday was too often an example of a theatrical one.

The other thing we should be clear about is that we are not trying to treat the whole fields of Homiletics and Theology. We shall assume that the sermon will be rooted deeply in a virile theology and that it will have a solid structure of thought. Our concern here is limited to suggestions, based on the dramatic art, of *communicating that thought with power* to lay men and women in the language of the heart.

1. The minister can learn from the dramatist to *think imaginatively;* that is, in images or pictures. Everyday people think in pictures, not in the abstractions of theologians. Anyone who hopes to influence the thinking of such everyday people must put his own thought in pictorial terms. But there are pictures and pictures. Some are as dull as abstractions. A picture must have life, action, emotion if it is to catch and hold the attention. This is the kind the dramatist uses. It is the kind Jesus used intuitively. The people who heard him saw in their mind's eyes the Prodigal Son asking his father for his inheritance, wasting it in riotous living, coming to grief and repentance as he was reduced to feeding pigs. They saw the boy returning to his father, and the father coming out gladly to meet him with open arms and a forgiving heart. There was life in that picture; there was struggle, emotion, and climax. In like manner the people saw the sower going forth to scatter his seed, and some of it falling on stony ground and some on fertile soil. They saw a shepherd seeking a lost sheep; a woman searching her house for a lost coin; a man burying his money in the ground, a woman leavening her bread; a merchant searching for a pearl of great price; a farmer contending with weeds planted by an enemy.

Note that all these pictures were *familiar* scenes to his audience. Someone had lost something precious and was trying to recover it. Or he was seeking something that would add to the fulness of life. Pictures of that sort always touch the human heart.

2. This brings us to the second thing the sermon-maker can learn from the dramatist: to present his thought not only in terms of pictures, but of *persons*. Not persons in the abstract, but flesh and blood characters convincing in their reality; persons whom the individuals in the congregation recognize as like unto themselves. When Henry Ward Beecher thundered against slavery, he dealt not only with

the system of slavery; he made people see slaves as human beings—fathers and mothers, boys and girls possessed of the same aspirations and emotions that belong to all humans. On one occasion he actually brought a colored girl into the pulpit and dramatized, before the congregation, a slave auction. His people never forgot that sermon. They may have forgotten his words, but not the picture of that suffering girl.

One of the sermons I shall longest remember was preached by the late Frank Gunsaulus of Chicago. He took as his text, "And Peter followed afar off." He began with a vivid characterization of Peter and by identifying *me* with that impulsive disciple who made such loud protestations of loyalty to the Master. Then he described Peter's cowardice in the hour of testing. In shame and penitence I saw myself, like Peter, denying my Lord, forsaking him, and then following him afar off, sneaking along in the shadows.

But Dr. Gunsaulus did not leave me there. He went on to draw the picture of another scene a few weeks later. I can still see it—that huge crowd gathered at Jerusalem listening in wonder and awe to a man of great power telling them that this Jesus whom they had crucified was his Lord and Master, and theirs too. He is calling them to take up his way of life. What courage this preacher has—what fire! He persuades three thousand to the cause of Christ that day of Pentecost. Yet this is the same Simon Peter who had followed Jesus afar off. After his repentance the grace of God had brought him new faith and courage. He had asserted the divine possibilities which had all the time been latent in his heart. Would I not let the grace of God work in me and let it bring out my possibilities?

As I walked home with a friend, I discovered that he, too, felt that Gunsaulus had identified him with Peter. Probably most of the congregation had the same experience and made the same re-dedication that we made. Here was a sermon that did not use a character as an illustration. The character *was* the sermon.

There is a vast difference between using a person as an illustration and using him as the source of the sermon. Both uses are legitimate, but the *source*-use has a significance and value less often realized. The difference is the difference between the word and the word-become-flesh. Various prophets of olden times had preached God's word with imaginative power through sermons, books, and other writings. Man heard—and forgot. But when God wanted to reveal Himself in a way that man could not forget, He sent "His only begotten son that whosoever believeth on him might not perish but have everlasting life." The word became flesh and dwelt among us. In this act God the creator became God the divine dramatist. When all the words of the prophets have been forgotten, the majestic yet humble figure of Christ will still live on, forever calling men to a new way of life.

The modern preacher can hardly be compared to God. But he can at least learn from God, and from lesser dramatists, this method of using persons as a source for sermons that live. He can find in the humblest layman, as well as in the most exalted saint, the revelation of God's way with men. The biographical sermon has not yet come into its own among us. It is a mine whose rich possibilities still await the explorations of the more adventurous.

In this connection, it might not be out of place to suggest that the minister would do well to draw most of his biographical sermons from lay men and women rather than from ministers. What would we think of a dramatist who always made the hero of his play a dramatist? Yet many preachers have confined their biographical sermons largely to ministers, missionaries, and other professional religious leaders. They have dealt with John Wesley, Phillips Brooks, Wilfred Grenfell, Albert Schweitzer, and Kagawa. They have neglected such significant scientists as Galileo, Isaac Newton, Darwin, Pasteur, Henri Fabre, E. L. Trudeau, William Osler, Sir Oliver Lodge, Michael Pupin, and Marie Curie. And such statesmen as William Penn, Benjamin Franklin, Thomas Jefferson, Edmund Burke, Wilberforce, Woodrow Wilson, and Lenin. And such artists as Leonardo, Michelangelo, Rembrandt, and Christopher Wren. And such musicians as Handel, Bach, Mozart, and Beethoven. And such writers as Dante, Milton, Locke, Samuel Johnson, Kant, Paine, Goethe, Wordsworth, Lamb, Hugo, Emerson, Tennyson, Dickens, Browning, George Eliot, Matthew Arnold, Dostoevsky, Ibsen, Tolstoy, William James, R. L. Stevenson, Galsworthy, and Masefield. And such leaders of business and of labor as Wanamaker of New York, Edward Filene of Boston, Robert Donnelly of Chicago, Keir Hardie of England, George Eastman of Rochester, Samuel Gompers and Charles Stelzle of America. And there is still the unnamed host of lesser-known men and women in every region and century.

Someone may object that these laymen were not as saintly as the ministers and missionaries. Perhaps not. But since when has God confined his revelations to the saints? Was Peter a saint? or James? or John? or any other disciple of Jesus? Thank Heaven God speaks to us through sinners as well as through saints. Moreover—and this is the essential point —the members of the congregation are lay men and women; they are employers or employees, farmers or mechanics, from forty to sixty hours each week. In their off hours many of them at least find release and re-creation in music and art, science and literature. They are naturally more interested in people who have faced their daily problems. The minister who preaches a larger proportion of his sermons about laymen, may hear rising from his congregation sighs of relief and gratitude.

3. He may learn, too, the value of presenting the persons

in his sermons in the midst of a *struggle*. It will be a struggle or conflict common to the experience of his congregation. A play without a struggle running all through it would fall flat. The central character in a good play wants something. He knows what he wants and sets out to get it. But he is opposed by someone else, or by a whole group, or by the circumstances of his life. All this is the common experience of every worthy life. The people in the audience of the theater are concerned with that struggle and the persons in it to the degree that it reflects the struggle that they themselves have faced. It may be the struggle for love, or for security, or for an education, or for reconciliation, or for justice. Whatever it is, it must contain some elements of universality and of significance if it is to hold the interest of the audience for two hours.

Here the minister whose pastoral work has made him familiar with the deeper conflicts in the lives of his people should have little trouble. He need not invent a struggle. There before him on Sunday morning sit scores or hundreds of human beings whose lives are filled with struggle. He will not betray any confidence, but he knows they have come in the hope that he will throw some light upon their path. Quietly they wait for him to give them courage, strength, insight, understanding—something that will help them and guide them in the decisions they must make. Many of them live upon the edge of tragedy. A false step, a mistaken judgment, a wrong decision, an ungenerous act may send them over the brink of that tragedy this coming week. The minister who forgets these struggling souls and fails to extend that understanding and shed upon their struggles the spiritual light they need fails in his highest function as a servant of God. On the other hand, the minister who builds his sermons around their struggles, presents them honestly and sympathetically, and brings to them the perspectives of eternity and the resources of a living faith, may be sure that though his words falter, they will carry the message of God and his people will go out from the church doors with new hope in their hearts.

4. If the minister portrays a human struggle in his sermon he will find another skill of the dramatist useful: building that struggle to a *climax,* holding the issue in *suspense* until the climax is reached. The dramatist does this by making the opposing forces in the struggle so evenly balanced that no one can be sure how the battle is coming out. Step by step, episode by episode, he builds the interest in that struggle. First the protagonist seems to have a clear right of way. Then the antagonist appears and disputes it. The protagonist seeks help; but the antagonist also calls up reserves, and again they contend. One side wins a minor engagement, but the other side wins the next. The more opposition the protagonist meets, the more the sympathy of the audience is stirred in his behalf. So it goes until all the forces on both sides have been marshaled and concentrated on the one big "obligatory scene" where the decisive choice must be made and the victory won or lost. That moment of decision, when the emotions of the audience are most deeply involved, is the climax. It is a difficult art—building such a climax and holding the interest in suspense—and few ministers seem to attempt it. But it might be worth trying. Not so many of the congregation would be caught napping, or glancing at their watches.

5. Whether or not a minister learns from the dramatist how to build his sermon into a climactic structure, there can be no question that he will want to apply to his sermon the test that every drama must meet: does it reach the *emotions?* The logic of the sermon may be faultless, its scientific data accurate, its biblical text and references unassailable, its diction impeccable—but if the sum total does not succeed in moving at least a part of the congregation to feel deeply,

the sermon is as flat and unprofitable as a drama that never stirs the heart. That deep feeling may be a sense of exaltation as one is lifted into the presence of God. It may be a sense of fellowship with a larger group of human beings than one has ever known. It may be a sense of awe at the mystery of divine forgiveness for one's sins. It may be a sense of gratitude for the redeeming grace of Christ. It may be such a stirring of the rebel passion of pity that one resolves to do something to secure justice for the oppressed. It may be any one of a score of emotions—but unless it touches one or more of them and kindles it to flame, the congregation is left cold. Bearing down on the conscience is not enough. The minister must also lift up the heart.

Here the minister faces a danger. It is the danger of dishonesty, the same danger the dramatist faces in building his climax. The emotion of the sermon, and the emotion of the drama, must be honest, not counterfeit. It must touch deep sentiment, not simply stir up superficial sentimentality. The preacher who "bores for water"—that is, tries to bring tears to the eyes of the congregation by some such device as parading his dead mother or theirs across the platform, is as much a faker as the dramatist who tries to bolster his play by introducing a parade of soldiers marching behind Old Glory while children sing "God Bless America." Real emotion cannot be injected like a shot in the arm. It must be the inevitable outcome of the sympathetic portrayal of the human struggle upon which the minister has endeavored to shed spiritual light. If he has drawn his struggle from the daily lives of his people, if he has brought to bear upon it the deeper insights of religion, he needs no artificial stimulus to reach the emotions. They will rise to meet his message as naturally as the flowers lift their opening petals to the summer sun.

Summing it up, then, these are some of the elements of

human interest the minister can learn from the dramatist for the building of a sermon: To think in terms of pictures, and especially pictures of flesh and blood persons. To portray those persons in the midst of some struggle common to the experience or observation of the congregation. To build that struggle to a climax and to aim throughout the sermon to reach not the intellect only but the deep emotional springs of feeling and action.

## VI

We turn now to the question: What can the minister learn from the dramatist concerning the conduct of a service of worship? The word "worship," according to the Encyclopedia Britannica, is a contraction of "worth-ship." It connotes an appreciation of worth or value. In religious usage it means an act or service in which a person seeks to appreciate and give honor to the highest of all values known to man: God.

Put in simple terms, the goal of the Protestant worship service is to bring the human into touch with the divine, the creature into fellowship with his creator. If it succeeds in this the human sees his littleness against God's greatness, his material ambitions against God's spiritual purposes, his temporal values against God's eternal ones; his sinfulness against God's righteousness. And the human cries, "Create in me a clean heart, O God, and renew a right spirit within me!" Cleansed, refreshed, strengthened, he goes out into the world to serve God and his brother men. Let us keep this goal of worship in mind as we seek to discover what the minister can learn from the dramatist in producing such an effect.

1. He can learn what the dramatist himself has had to learn about judging his drama by its *total effect* upon the audience. Not the effect of one scene or one act, but the combined effect of the whole play upon the audience. So with a service of worship. It should be a unit designed to weld a

heterogeneous aggregation of individuals into a fellowship with each other and with God. They come from many homes and conditions of life. They come with a variety of troubles and cares and worries. The service should lift them gradually out of the little things that divide them and into the high plane where they feel their oneness and see life in the long perspectives of spiritual religion. Across the doorway of the First Unitarian Church of Chicago the minister, Dr. Von Ogden Vogt, has had carved where those who enter from the street may see them these words: "Out of the World of the Many into the World of the One." As the congregation leaves they can see over the same doorway, on the inside, these words: "Out of the World of the One into the World of the Many." Every minister who knows what worship is tries to make those words a reality. He tries to send the people away with a feeling of oneness with God and each other that they will carry with them through the week ahead.

To make this more graphic, suppose we take the case of one man—let us call him John Goodman. Let us assume that he is a fairly typical church member who recognizes that there is something in life beyond business and pleasure, something of a spiritual nature which his church tries to cultivate. Let us assume further, that he has come into church on a Sunday morning and has taken his seat in his usual pew. As he sits there his mind is still occupied with his problems of the past week. His children are growing up and he is concerned that they become of good character and intelligence and that they honor their parents and develop into useful citizens. His older son, Edward, is in the navy, but no word has been heard from him for months. Haunting John's mind is the fear that a telegram may come any day now—a telegram he will be afraid to open. Meanwhile there is his daughter, Mary. Lately she has taken to running around with a young blade who seems to have nothing to commend him but a handsome face and curly hair. Certainly, according to John, he has neither sense nor manners. And there is considerable doubt about his morals. What should a father do? Then there is his son, David, just turned eighteen. David is a good boy, but the Government has decreed that the army must have him. He's a sensitive young fellow with a taste for literature and art. Some day he might be a writer, or an editor, or at least a teacher. He was all set for entering John's old college—but now the army has called him. What if he should be injured—or worse? And what will the military life do to his mind and his sense of values? Of course John wants to do the right thing for his country—but is this it? John's wife has been worrying about these things, too, and the worry has increased the strain on her already poor health. Something must be done for that good woman—but what? And as for his business—what with the new government restrictions, priorities, and his inability to get materials—where is he coming out? These are but a few of the things in John Goodman's mind as the service begins.

Now the minister knows John. He wants this service to help him. He can't expect to solve John's problems. But he does hope to make this service so helpful that John will go away with new courage, a stronger faith, and a deepened sense of brotherhood with other human beings facing similar problems. The minister has prepared his sermon to that end. But this sermon is but one factor in the worship service. How can the other factors be so united with it that the whole service will have the desired effect?

2. The minister may learn from the dramatist—or from the theater which brings to life the dramatist's play—the *importance of the physical factors* in John Goodman's environment during the next hour. For if his pew is uncomfortable, if the air he breathes is foul or draughty, if the lights of the church glare in his eyes, if the noises of the street or the

adjoining room distract his attention, the ministries of music and preaching will be handicapped, if not frustrated. The theater—even the small local movie—long since learned that the drama will have a better chance to register upon the mind and heart of John Goodman if his body is comfortably situated in a room with soft lighting and adequate ventilation. A large proportion of the theaters today are air conditioned. Not so the average church. The air there is best described by the old quatrain—some like it hot, some like it cold, some like it in the church seven days old. The theater provides John Goodman with a seat that distributes his weight fairly equally all the way from the knee to the shoulder. The church thus far has scorned any knowledge of such scientific seating. In the average pew the weight of the body rests altogether on the base of the spine—a position that can hardly be borne comfortably for more than an hour and a quarter. That is one reason, at least, why a theater can hold its audience for more than two hours without complaint, whereas the church has found that any service lasting over an hour and a quarter, runs into collision with the law of diminishing returns.

Of these various physical factors, lighting is perhaps the most important. Church lighting should be designed as a positive aid to worship. Instead it is usually designed only to illuminate a room.

A few years ago I published a few paragraphs in the *Christian Century* asking the readers if they were satisfied with the lighting in their churches. If not, would they write me letters about it? More than two hundred of them wrote letters saying *no,* they were not satisfied. They said their lighting was often more of a hindrance than a help to worship. It glared. It showed up the freckles of the congregation but left the altar in darkness. It was static, not mobile. Its operation was by abrupt and noisy switches. It attracted attention to itself rather than to the places where that attention was desired. It illuminated the wrong parts of the room, and it did nothing to aid the mood of devotion and worship. It usually left the minister's face in shadow. What did they want in the way of improved lighting? They said they wanted light that performed its function so effectively that no one ever thought about it. All wanted their lighting improved; and they were equally unanimous at another point: the improvements should not be expensive.

Therefore, in an effort to give some sort of practical guidance to these churches that wanted better lighting, I sought out a few capable lighting engineers and architects and together we worked out a plan. We agreed that lighting designed to be a positive aid to worship means lighting that makes the congregation feel that it is in a place of beauty and peace. More than that, it means lighting that quietly and without ostentation focuses the attention of the congregation just where that attention is desired at any given moment in the service—now upon the altar, now upon the choir, now upon the minister, and now upon the hymn books of the people in the pews.[4]

---

4 To achieve such lighting we agreed that the following were the minimum requirements.

In every church auditorium, large or small, there should be at least three lighting circuits; one for the auditorium as a whole, one for the chancel and choir, one for the pulpit. Many churches will need a fourth circuit to be used independently to illuminate the altar or communion table.

Each of these should be controlled by switches equipped with dimmers so that the intensity of the light may be varied in accordance with the need, gradually and without sharp or abrupt change.

All the switches and dimmers should be operated from a single switchboard located near the organist, who should be responsible for regulating the light as the service progresses. Light and music are both essential for developing the proper mood; they should work in harmony and not against each other. The organist will need to shift the lighting only three or four times during the service, and a moment's attention in each case is all that will be required of him.

At the beginning of the service the auditorium or nave should be dimly lighted and the chancel and altar emphasized; when the hymns are sung

3. Finally, the minister can learn from the dramatist that the profound spiritual lift he seeks for the soul of John Goodman is not to be attained at a single bound. He reaches it through a *progression of emotions*. The dramatist would plan to lead John Goodman from thinking solely about his own troubles by interesting him in the troubles of similar characters in the play. As the play progresses, John in the theater would pass through a series of emotions by which he gradually transfers his pity and fear for himself to pity and fear for some character in the drama. That transference of pity and fear from self to someone else is as we have seen the exalted use of those emotions which, according to Aristotle, produces a catharsis, a spiritual cleansing.

Just so the minister will plan his worship service to lead John Goodman through a series of such emotions as gratitude, penitence, aspiration, compassion, hope, and courage. With the coöperation of the choir director, he will plan the music, prayers, responses, sermon, and benediction to work in harmony to this end. He will not allow the sequence of emotions to be interrupted by announcements or anything else that breaks the progression. Every such break destroys in some measure the emotional continuity. He will no more break that continuity than the dramatist would interrupt his play to make announcements about even such worthy objects as Community Chest and Red Cross drives (Plate XXIV B).

Let us suppose that John Goodman's minister has planned his sermon and his service of worship with these principles

---

the lights in the auditorium should be fully lighted, then dimmed during the prayer, the anthem, and the sermon. The lights upon the choir should be brought up when it sings and dimmed afterward. The lights upon the pulpit should be intensified when the minister is reading or addressing the congregation.

Such lighting need not be expensive; in fact it should be less so than the older type that required heavy and costly chandeliers which attracted attention to themselves and contributed little or nothing to the beauty of the service.

in mind. Let us suppose further that with the help of the church officers, the physical environment of John Goodman and the other members of the congregation has been so carefully prepared that it works with the service and not against it. The pews are comfortable, the air fresh and at the right temperature, the whole atmosphere of the church one of peace and beauty. What happens to John and his mental burden of worry and care?

Picture him as he takes his seat. The lights gently guide his attention to the softly lighted altar. The organist finishes the prelude. The choir, singing the processional hymn of praise, moves down the aisle and into its stalls. As the singers take their places their faces are illuminated by the concealed chancel lights. The minister invokes the blessing of God. Choir and congregation lift their voices in response, closing with the prayer John learned in his childhood—"Our Father, who art in heaven . . ." John begins to feel less alone. Others all around him also learned that prayer in their childhood. They, too, know the uncertainties and sorrows of an imperfect world and are praying "Thy Kingdom come, thy will be done on earth as it is in heaven. . . ."

In the anthem, the scripture reading, and the hymns that follow, John is led step by step out of the world of the many into the world of the One, up from the valley of shadow and worry and doubt, up to the hilltop of vision where he sees life in its long perspective. He is not the first to have struggled through that valley and up that hill. The children of Israel long ago made that journey. They, too, had sinned and done that which was evil in the sight of the Lord. The Lord had chastised them but forgiven them. When they fainted he had lifted them up and set their feet upon the way of righteousness and peace. He had taught them to distil power out of their pain, and to learn mercy through their suffering.

The early Christians who carried the message of Jesus
beyond the tiny province of Galilee out into the Roman
world with all its tyrannical cruelty, had known every hard-
ship that a military dictatorship could inflict upon them to
break their spirits. They had borne all the griefs that John
Goodman bears, and more. They had suffered persecution;
their families had been torn apart, their sons killed.

In the pastoral prayer the minister gives thanks for this
heritage of courage, seeks forgiveness for the sins that have
brought new calamities upon the world, remembers those
who are bearing crosses today in body, mind, or spirit, petitions for strength and courage to meet the individual needs
of the congregation and the social needs of a generation
striving to find a way out of its welter of blood into an era
of peace and goodwill.

The choir takes up the theme and on the wings of music
lifts its appeal—

> Spirit Divine, attend our prayer,
>   Make a lost world thy home;
> Descend with all thy gracious power,
>   Come, Holy Spirit, come!

And now the minister is preaching. It is a sermon that
begins with one of the conflicts that has so worn the heart
of John Goodman. A sermon peopled with men like himself.
It goes on to set these men in the larger struggle that has
been going on for centuries—the struggle of transforming
the chaos of the world into order, its stagnation into growth,
its hatred into love, its ugliness into beauty, its warfare into
peace. Scene by scene the sermon rises to its climax. John
Goodman sees his own life set in that larger perspective. He
feels his kinship with those imperfect men who had striven
as he has striven and had known defeat. But he also sees
himself akin with those who, laying hold on God, had risen

from their defeats, asserted new courage, and cried with Saint Paul, "We are troubled on every side, yet not distressed; we are perplexed, but not in despair; persecuted, but not forsaken; cast down, but not destroyed . . ."

The sermon is finished, the lights come up on the altar and chancel. The benediction is pronounced, the choral "Amen" sung. A bell sounds softly. Gradually the lights in the auditorium come up. The service is over. John Goodman, exalted in spirit, goes out into the world to take up his daily cross. And in his heart there is a new sense of fellowship with God and his fellow men.

# Bibliography

*Fifteen Greek Plays,* translated into English by Gilbert Murray, Benjamin Bickley Rogers, and others. With a supplement from the "Poetics of Aristotle" by Lane Cooper. New York: Oxford University Press, 1943.
Four plays by Sophocles; four by Aeschylus; four by Euripides; and three by Aristophanes.

Barrett H. Clark (Compiler): *World Drama.* 2 vols. New York: D. Appleton-Century Company, 1933.
Carefully selected collection of plays of ancient Greece, Rome, India, China, Japan; Medieval Europe and England; and Modern Italy, Spain, France, Germany, Denmark, Russia, and Norway.

Nellie B. Miller: *The Living Drama.* New York: D. Appleton-Century Company. 1924
An admirable and brief outline of the history of drama in the western world.

Bernard Shaw: *Nine Plays.* New York: Dodd, Mead and Company, 1935
Some of his best work, including "Saint Joan," "Candida," and "The Devil's Disciple."

John Galsworthy: *Representative Plays*. New York: Charles
     Scribner's Sons, 1924
     Includes "Strife," "Justice," "Loyalties," and three others
     together with an introduction by George Pierce Baker.

*The Theatre Guild Anthology*. New York: Random House, 1936
     Includes fourteen plays "as a representative cross-section of
     the Guild's scope and activities" since its founding in 1918.
     One play from each of the following authors: St. John G.
     Ervine, A. A. Milne, Ferenc Molnar, Leonid Andreyev, Elmer
     Rice, Bernard Shaw, Franz Werfel, Sidney Howard, Dorothy
     and DuBose Heyward, Eugene O'Neill, Philip Barry, Robert
     E. Sherwood, Maxwell Anderson, and S. N. Behrman.

### COLLECTIONS OF ONE-ACT RELIGIOUS PLAYS

Laurence Housman: *Little Plays of St. Francis*. Boston: Walter
     H. Baker Company, 1935
     St. Francis of Assisi in a cycle of plays from legendary sources
     and from the records of history.

Fred Eastman: *Plays of American Life*. New York: Samuel French,
     1934
     One three-act and seven one-act plays, each centering around
     a modern social and spiritual conflict in American life. Includes
     "The Tinker," "The Great Choice," "Bread," "Our Lean
     Years," "The Doctor Decides," "The Ragged Edge," "Court-
     ship."

———— (ed.): *Ten One-act Plays*. Chicago: Willett, Clark and
     Company, 1937
     Themes of social significance: war and peace, loyalty, beauty
     amid squalor, nationalism versus religion, Christmas in the
     modern world. The volume includes: "Monsignor's Hour,"
     by Emmet Lavery; "Pawns," by Percival Wilde; "Prize Money,"
     by Louis Wilson; "The Great Choice," by Fred Eastman; "He
     Came Seeing," by Mary P. Hamlin; "Tidings of Joy," by
     Elizabeth McFadden; "The Tail of the Dragon," by Elliot
     Field; "The Lord's Prayer," by François Coppee; "Twentieth
     Century Lullaby," by Cedric Mount; "Peace I Give Unto
     You," by Dorothy Clarke Wilson. A survey of the nature and
     extent of the use of religious drama in the United States is
     appended.

Fred Eastman (ed.): *Modern Religious Dramas.* New York: Harper and Bros., 1938. Includes "Neighbors" by Zona Gale, "Confessional" by Percival Wilde, "What Men Live By" by Virginia Church, "The Valiant" by Hall and Middlemass, "Bread" by Fred Eastman, "The Deathless World" by J. M. S. Thompkins, "El Cristo" by Margaret Larkin, "Dust of the Road" by Kenneth Sawyer Goodman, "The Color Line" by Irene Taylor MacNair, and "The Pageant of the Holy Grail" by W. Russell Bowie.

## A MANUAL

Fred Eastman and Louis Wilson: *Drama in the Church.* New York: Samuel French, 1933; Revised 1942.

Sums up briefly the most important things drama groups should know for the task of producing plays in churches, not as entertainment, but as a means of ministering to the souls of men through a great art.

# INDEX OF PERSONS

Abraham, 49, 51
Achaeans, 39
Adam, 53
Adams, Henry, 59
Aeschylus, 137, 146
Allah, 14
Ambrose of Milan, 100
Amitaba Buddha, 49
Amon, 5, 36
Amos, 20, 63
Anderson, Marian, 23
Anderson, Maxwell, 138, 150
Andromeda, 45
Angelico, Fra, 6, 53, 58, 67
Antichrist, 54
Apollo, 20
Aphrodite, 41
Aristotle, 147, 164
Arnold, Matthew, 155
Asoka, 14
Athena, 14, 20, 39, 41, 45
Atlas, 40
Augustine, 98, 112

Baals, 6
Bach, 6, 25, 93, 96, 102, 112, 119, 120, 155
Bailey, Albert E., 34
Barnby, Joseph, 121
Barry, Philip, 138
Beach, Mrs. H. H. A., 123
Beaven, Pres. Albert, 25
Beecher, Henry Ward, 152
Beethoven, 96, 100, 102, 119, 155
Behrman, S. N., 138
Beneker, Gerrit, 64, 65
Benson, Dr. Louis, 109
Benton, Thomas, 64
Billings, William, 93, 122
Binyon, Laurence, 61
Blake, William, 59, 62
Blow, John, 120

Bodhisattvas, 56
Borluut, Elizabeth, 61
Bortniansky, 101
Bourgeois, Louis, 22, 116
Brahms, 102
Bramante, 76
Breasted, James H., 13n, 19
Brooks, Phillips, 154
Browning, 155
Buck, Dudley, 123
Buddha, 14, 44
    See also Amitaba, Gautama
Buddhas, 56
Burke, Edmund, 155
Bushman, 4
Byrd, William, 112, 120
Byzantines, 77, 78, 80

Calvin, 22, 93, 115, 116
Cezanne, 63
Charlemagne, 81
Chartran, Théobald, 11
Cherubim, 37
Cho-Shi-Kio, 37
Christiansen, F. Meluis, 123
Chrysostom, 98
Clark, Jeremiah, 120
Clement of Alexandria, 96
Cleopatra, 98
Clovis, 80
Columbus, 122
Conant, Kenneth J., 13, 15, 18, 70
Connelly, Marc, 28
Constantine, 15, 18, 51, 57, 73, 74
Coomaraswamy, Ananda, 56n
Copeland, Aaron, 128
Cosimo de' Medici, 53
Cowper, 99
Cranach, Lucas, 54, 55
Croft, William, 120
Curie, Marie, 155

171

Cybele, 20
Cyprian, St., 51

Dali, Salvador, 8
Danaans, 39
Daniel, 51
Dante, 155
Darwin, 155
David, 6
Davison, Archibald, 99n, 121
Deborah, 20
Dewey, John, 136
Dickens, 155
Dickinson, Clarence, 123
Diocletian, 73, 77
Dionysius the Younger, 98
Dionysus, 6, 137, 146
Donnelly, Robert, 155
Dostoevsky, 155
Douglas, Canon, 123
Duns Scotus, 54
Dürer, 52, 54
Dykes, John Bacchus, 121

Eastman, Fred, 25, 26, 28, 134
Eastman, George, 155
Eliot, George, 155
Elizabeth I, 22
Elvey, George, 121
Emerson, 155
Euripides, 137
Eusebius, 57
Eyck, van, 42, 60

Fabian Society, 27
Fabre, Henri, 155
Filene, Edward, 155
Fosdick, Harry Emerson, 137, 151
Francis, St., 11
Franck, César, 102, 119
Franklin, Benjamin, 155
Franks, 80

Galileo, 155
Galsworthy, John, 27, 142–150, 155
Ganesha, 36
Garuda, 36
Gautama Buddha, 50
Gebhardt, Edouard, 59

Geer, Will, 128
Gesner, 119
Gibbons, Orlando, 120
Giotto, 10
Glinker, 101
Goering, 61
Goes, van der, 52
Goethe, 155
Gompers, 155
Goss, John, 121
Goya, 63
Greco, El, 8
Green, Paul, 138
Gregory the Great, 6, 100, 111
Gregory of Tours, 81
Grenfel, Wilfred, 154
Gretchaninoff, 101, 109
Grieg, 105
Gunsaulus, Frank, 153

Handel, 93, 96, 99, 102, 155
Hanuman, 36
Hardie, Keir, 155
Harker, F. F., 123
Harwood, Basil, 123
Hassler, Hans Leo, 115
Hathor, 17, 36, 48
Haydn, 96, 118
Heliogabolus, 98
Herakles, 40, 44
Hermes, 20, 41, 45
Hindus, 37
Hi-yi-shon-a-gu, 36
Hocking, William E., 3–4
Hoffman, Irwin, 65
Holbein the Younger, 54
Holst, Gustav, 123
Holt, Arthur, 30, 31
Horus, 5, 16, 17, 36
Hugo, 155
Hunefer, 10
Hunt, W. Holman, 59

Ibsen, 27, 155
Indians, American, 4
Ippolitof-Ivanoff, 101
Ireland, John, 123
Isaac, 51
Isaiah, 52

Isis, 50
Israelites (Israel), 19, 20, 63

Jacob, 14, 15
James, William, 10, 155
Jefferson, Thomas, 155
Jesus, 135
John of Damascus, 101
Johnson, Samuel, 155
Jonah, 54
Jones, E. Stanley, 24
Joseph, St., 53
Justinian, 18, 51, 78, 80
Justus of Ghent, 52

Kagawa, 154
Kant, 155
Kastalsky, 101
Kheper, 36
Kingsley, Sidney, 138, 150
Kinlock, T. F., 121

Lamb, 155
Lanier, Sidney, 62
Lao-Tzu, 61
Lavington, 99
Lenin, 155
Leonardo, 155
Lincoln, 128–130
Locke, 155
Lodge, Sir Oliver, 155
Longfellow, 7
Luccock, Halford, 136
Luther, 21, 26, 54, 93, 114, 115

Macfarlane, Will C., 123
Maderna, 76
Marsh, Reginald, 65
Marsyas, 20
Martin, George, 121
Martin, Jacques, 65
Martin, Paul, 128
Martin, Quinquela, 66
Mary, Bloody, 22
Mary the Virgin (Madonna), 8, 51, 52, 53, 59, 60, 99
Masefield, 155
Mason, Lowell, 93, 122
Mendelssohn, 96
Messiah, 53

Methodists, 27
Meyer, Henry H., 117n
Michelangelo, 10, 42, 43, 76, 155
Milton, John, 42, 155
Minotaur, 45
Miriam, 19
Mnemosyne, 20
Molina-Campos, 62
Moltke, Count von, 101
Moody, Dwight L., 93
Moravians, 116
Moses, 50
Moustapha, Kemel, 20
Mozart, 96, 155
Muses, 20

Navajo sand painter 55
Nero, 98
Newton, Isaac, 155
Noah, 50, 51
Noble, T. Tertius, 123

O'Neill, Eugene, 138, 150
Origen, 57
Orozco, José, 65
Orpheus, 45
Osiris, 10, 14, 26, 48
Osler, William, 155
Ouseley, Frederick, 121

Paine, Thomas, 155
Palestrina, 6, 93, 112, 113
Parker, Horatio, 123
Pasteur, 155
Paul, St., 45
Penn, William, 155
Perseus, 45
Peter, St., 45, 49
Phideas, 40, 41
Plato, 98
Pliny, 21
Portinari, Tommaso, 53
Praxiteles, 41
Priscilla, catacomb of, 52
Procopius, 79
Ptolemies, 98
Pupin, Michael, 155
Puritans, 22

Quakers, 98

Rachmaninoff, 101
Raemaekers, 64
Raphael, 12, 24, 52
Raven, the Old, 36
Raven, the Young, 36
Reeves, Jeremiah, 115
Rembrandt, 155
Rip van Winkle, 10
Rogers, James H., 123
Romans, 77, 80
Rossini, 98

Sankey, Ira D., 93
Santayana, 8
Sargent, John S., 8, 10
Sassoon, Siegfried, 124n
Schleiermacher, 104
Schongauer, 54
Schütz, Heinrich, 96
Schweitzer, Albert, 154
Semites, 6
Set, 5
Shakespeare, 148
Shaw, Geoffrey, 123
Shaw, George Bernard, 27
Shaw, Martin, 123
Sheehan, Vincent, 23
Shelley, Harry Rowe, 123
Sherwood, Robert, 138
Siddartha, Prince, (Buddha), 44
Siva, 38
Smith, H. Augustine, 25, 92
Sophocles, 137
Sowerby, Leo, 123
Spencer, Bishop, 96
Stainer, John, 121
Stanford, Charles V., 121
Stelzle, Charles, 155
Stevenson, R. L., 155
Stravinsky, Ivor, 111
Sullivan, Arthur, 121
Sunday, Billy, 151
Sung Dynasty, 61

Tao, 61
Tallis, Thomas, 120
Tennyson, 62, 155
Theseus, 45
Thracians, 45

Three Worthies, 50, 51
Tissa, 14
Titcomb, Everett, 123
Tissot, 59
Titzel, 54
Tolstoy, 65, 155
Trajan, 21
Trudeau, E. L., 155
Tschaikowsky, 101
Tschesnokoff, 101
Tucker, Bland, 96
Tufts, John, 122
Tyrell, George, 150

Uhde, Fritz, 59
Urbino, Duke of, 52

Venus, 5
Verestchagin, 64
Vogt, Von Ogden, 160
Voltaire, 6
Vydt, Judocus, 61

Wagner, 105
Wanamaker, 155
Watts, Isaac, 93
Wesley, John, 27, 154
Wesleys, the, 22
White, Andrew, 101
Whitefield, George, 22
Whitehead, Alexander, 123
Whittemore, Thomas, 79
Wilberforce, 155
Wilder, Thornton, 28, 138, 150
Wildex, Percival, 147
Willan, Healey, 123
Williams, David McK., 123
Williams, Ralph Vaughan, 123
Wilson, Woodrow, 155
Wohlgemut, 54
Woolley, Sir Leonard, 13, 19
Wordsworth, 62, 155
Wren Christopher, 155
Wright, George F., 101

Yahweh, 6, 19

Zen sect, 61
Zeus, 6, 20, 39, 41, 42
Zinzendorf, Count von, 116

# INDEX OF PLACES

Abbeville, 81
Abydos, 14, 26
Aegina, 39
Agra, 14
Alaska, 36
Alexandria, 46, 57, 81
Altamira, 6
Al-Urbaid, 19
Angkor Wat, 44
Antioch, 46, 51
Asia Minor, 20
Athens, 6, 14, 137

Baalbek, 75
Babylon, 54
Baltimore museum, 46
Berchières, 60
Bethel, 14
Bethlehem, 16
Borobudur, 44
Buddh-Gaya, 44
Buenos Aires, 66
Byzantium, 77
    See also Constantinople

Caesarea, 57
Calcedon, 51
Carmel, Mt., 4
Centula, 82
Ceylon, 14
Chartres, 59, 60
Chicago, 30
China, 4, 61
Cluny, 85, 86, 87
Constantinople (Istanbul), 15, 16, 18,
    46, 57, 77
Crete, 4

Dendera, 17
Dordogne, 3
Dresden, 12
Dura-Europos, 45

Egypt, 4, 13, 19, 26, 36
England, 22, 23, 27
Erech, 13

Florence, 53
France, 3, 60, 81

Gandhara, 44
Geneva, 22, 112, 115
Germany, 22, 53
Ghent, 42, 60
Greece, 20

Herrnhut, 116
Hollywood, 62
Homburi mountains, 55

India, 4, 14, 36, 44, 56
Isle of Wight, 24
Istanbul. See Constantinople
Italy, 4

Jerusalem, 16, 37

Kandy, Ceylon, 49
Kansas, 29
Kish, 13
Kishon river, 20

Laon, 86
Leipzig, 119
Libyan desert, 4
London, 22, 24

Mediterranean, 39
Mesopotamia, 4, 13, 47, 77
Mexico, 60
Mihintale, 14

Nile, 14

Padua, 10
Paris, 15, 25

Pearl Harbor, 64
Persia, 14, 40, 61
Pompeii, 46
Prague, 112
Princeton Univ. museum, 46

Quarr Abbey, 24

Red sea, 19
Rome, 16, 18, 45, 51, 52

St. Petersburg, 101
Salzburg, 23
Sanchi, 44
Santiago de Compostela, 15
    See Architecture
        Buildings
Scandinavia, 4

Scotland, 22, 93
South Africa, 4
Spain, 4, 15, 57, 64
Sudan, 55

Thebes, 5
Troy, 45

Urbino, 52

Warka, 13
Wittenberg, 112
Worcester Art museum, 46
Worcester First Baptist church, 47

Yucatan, 4

Zurich, 112

# ANALYTICAL INDEX

ART (General, Painting, Sculpture)
an instinctive activity, 3
prehistoric origin, 3
universality, 3–4
humanized and expanded by social
 development, 6, 39–41
viewed as a challenge, 7–8
an authentic expression of religion,
 9–12
 intellectual approach, 9–11
 emotional approach, 11–12
perpetual service of, 12
visualizes gods, 36–43
 forms socially conditioned, 41
visualizes religious persons, 44–7
 Bible illustrations, 46–7
visualizes dogma, 47–53
 the after life, 47–50
 Christian salvation, 50–1
 decisions of church councils, 51
 church festivals, 52
 transubstantiation, Trinity, 52
 incarnation, atonement, 52–3
as propaganda, 53–5
as "bhakti," 55–62
opposition of the church, 57
Bible illustration as "bhakti," 58–9
as mystic interpretation of nature,
 61–2
as social criticism, 63–6

*Specific Works of Painting and
Sculpture*
 Adoration of the Lamb, Van Eyck,
  42, 60
 Adoration of Shepherds, 52–3
 Again, Thomas Benton, 64
 Apotheosis of War, Verestchagin,
  64
 Ascent to Heaven, Mirak, 44
 Athena, 39–40

*Specific Works of Painting and
Sculpture (Cont.)*:
 Bibles, illustrated
  Codex Rossano, 46
  Cotton Genesis, 46
  Cranach-Luther, 55
  Job, Book of, Blake, 59
  Joshua, Book of, 46
  Octateuch, 46
  Paris Psalter, 46
  Rabula Gospels, 47
  Septuagint, 46, 55
 Book of the Dead, 47
 Catacomb frescoes, 45
 Creation of Adam, Michelangelo, 42
 Crucifixion, Fra Angelico, 52
 Dance of Siva, 38
 Deposition, Fra Angelico, 6
 Disputa, Raphael, 52
 Enthroned Virgin, St. Sophia, 51
 Francis, St., Singing, Chartran, 11
 Going Forth by Day, papyrus, 48
 Healing the Paralytic, Dura-Euro-
  pos, 45
 Heaven, Chinese, 49
 Hell, Buddhist, 49
 Homecoming of the Workers,
  Orozco, 65
 Last Judgement, Bourges cathe-
  dral, 49
 Last Judgement, Michelangelo, 10,
  49
 Last Supper, Justus of Ghent, 52
 Men are Square, Beneker, 65
 Minorities, Gropper, 65
 Parable of the Two Houses, wood-
  cut, 54
 Passion Series, Dürer, 54
 Passion Series, Schongauer, 54
 Passion Series, Wohlgemut, 54
 Peacock King of Light, Cho-Shi-
  Kio, 37

177

Specific Works of Painting and
Sculpture (*Cont.*):
  Prehistoric rock paintings, 4, 5
  Rakan, Chinese, 44
  Ramayana illustrations, 44
  Reindeer, prehistoric engraving, 3
  Rubbish, Hoffman, 65
  Sistine Madonna, Raphael, 12
  "This is her first lynching," Marsh,
    65
  Totem pole, Alaska, 36
  Venus of Willendorf, 3
  Weighing of the Soul, papyrus, 10
  Wheel of the Law, Buddhist, 50

ARCHITECTURE
  younger than sculpture and paint-
    ing, 13
  served religion from the first, 13
  for remembrance, 14
  as God's house, 15, 16, 17
  for communal worship, 15
  symbol of imperial power, 15, 16, 74
  conditioned by ritual requirements,
    16
  Christian sublimation of old func-
    tions, 17, 18
  medieval, revival of interest in, 71
  medieval lost monuments, 72
  Early Christian, 73–77
    earliest buildings destroyed, 73
    development under Constantine,
      73–6
    quality of monumentality, 73–4
  Byzantine, 77–80
    quality of permanence, 77
    distinctive features, 77–8
    use of light, 79
    acoustics, 80
  Romanesque, 80–6
    quality of dramatic composition,
      80, 82
    distinctive features, 81–2
  Gothic, 86–8
    crown of long development, 72
    borrowed elements, 86
    distinctive features, 86
    quality of aspiration, 87–8

Specific Buildings
  basilica of Constantine, Rome, 87
  churches:
    Beauvais, 87–8
    Centula, monastery, 18, 81–2
    Chartres, 18, 87–8
    Cluny, 18, 85, 86, 87
    Gerona, 87
    Martyrion, Jerusalem, 16
    Nativity, Bethlehem, 16
    Notre Dame, Paris, 25, 87
    St. Bénigne, Dijon, 18, 83, 84, 85
    Ste. Chapelle, Paris, 15
    St. Denis, 86
    St. Irene (Holy Peace), Constan-
      tinople, 16
    St. James, Santiago de Compo-
      stela, 15, 18, 83, 84
    St. Martin, Tours, 81, 83
    St. Peter's (Old), Rome, 16, 18,
      74–6
    St. Requier. See Centula
    St. Sophia (Holy Wisdom), Con-
      stantinople, 15, 16, 18, 42,
      78–80, 87
  dagobas, Mihintale, 14
  Pharos, Alexandria, 81
  Taj Mahal, 14
  temples:
    Baalbek, 75
    Horus, Edfu, 16
    Mayan pyramid, 4
    Osireion, Abydos, 14
    Pantheon, Rome, 87
    Parthenon, 14
    Solomon, Jerusalem, 6
  Terraced pyramid, Sakkara, 13

MUSIC
  an instinctive activity, 18
  earliest instruments, 19
  primitive connection with religion,
    19–20
  in Greek mythology, 20
  earliest Christian, 21
  linked with religious vitality, 21–2
    in Germany, 21
    in England, 22
  releases emotion 23

Music (*Cont.*):
our response conditioned by concomitants, 23
specific emotions illustrated, 23–5
summary of history, 93–4
debt to the church, 94–5
contribution to the church, 96
religious differentiated from
churchly, 96–7, 99
subject to debasement, 97–9
tonal structure: 100–105
melody, 100
scales, 100–1
harmony and counterpoint, 101–2
rhythm, 102–4
tempo, 104–5
expression, 106–110
affected by architecture and liturgy, 106
five acts in ideal service, 107–110
masters and schools, 110–121
Hebrew, 110–1
Gregorian 111, 120
polyphonic, 112–3
Luther, 114–5
Calvin-Bourgeois, 115–6
Moravian, 116–7
function of choirs, 117–121
authorities quoted, 119–120
the Oxford movement, 121
religious music in America, 121–3
low grade, 122
early masters, 122
anthem writers and tone poets,
123
practical suggestions, 123–130
thirteen rules of universal song,
124–8
interrelation of music and speech,
128

*Musical Works*
Agnus Dei, 96
Benedictus, 96
Benedictus es Domini, 108
Cavalleria Rusticana, 97
Cherubic Hymn, 105
Creation, 96
Credo, 96

*Musical Works* (*Cont.*):
Elijah, 96
Fifth Symphony, 100
Gloria in Excelsis, 96
Gloria, Patri, 108
Gospodi Pomolui, 109
Hallel, the, 21
Hallelujah Chorus, 102
Hansel and Gretel, 97
Kyrie eleison, 96, 109
L'Arlesienne, 97
Litany, the, 24
Messiah, 96, 99
Metrical Psalms, 22
Miserere Domini, 109
Miserere Nobis, 109
O Lord have mercy, 109
Passion music, Bach, 6
St. Paul, 96
Sanctus, 96
Seven Words from the Cross, 96
Stabat Mater, 98
Sylvia, 97
Symphony in C minor, Beethoven,
102
Symphony in C minor, Brahms,
102
Symphony in D minor, Franck, 102
Tales of Hoffman, 97
Tannhäuser, 97
Thaïs, 97
Anthems:
Beloved, let us love one another,
Foote, 109
Come ye faithful, Titcomb, 108
God so loved the world, Stainer,
109
Ho, every one that thirsteth,
Martin, 109
O sing unto the Lord, Purcell, 108
Sing Alleluia forth, Thiman, 108
With a voice of singing, Shaw, 108
Chorale tunes:
Coelites plaudant, 100
Ein feste Burg, 21
Lasset uns erfreuden, 100
Lobe den Herren, 100
Old Hundreth, 100
Nun danket alle Gott, 100

*Musical Works (Cont.):*
 Hymn Tunes:
  Aberystwyth, 102
  Duke Street, 100
  God rest you merry, gentlemen, 102
  Hanover, 100, 103
  Leoni (Yigdal), 102
  Llangloffan, 102
  Lyons, 103
  Rockingham, 100
  St. Anne, 100
  St. Margaret, 103
  St. Thomas, 100
  Sine Nomine, 100
  Tallis' Canon, 100
  Ton-Y-Botel, 102
 Plainsong (Gregorian):
  Alla Trinita Beata, 100
  Divinum Mysterium, 100
  Veni Emmanuel, 100
 Spirituals:
  "And he never said a mumblin' word," 23
  "Were you there when they crucified my Lord," 24

DRAMA
 Dr. Eastman's point of view, 26
 earliest connection with religion, 26
  Mystery Play of Osiris, 26
  Miracle Plays, 26
 debauched in Restoration days, 26-7
 as social criticism, 27-8
 a technique for education, 28-30
 a technique for solving social conflicts, 30-1
 relation of religion to drama, 135
  religion must be dramatized, 135-6
 what dramatist and minister have in common, 136-9
  history, 136-7
  aims, 138
  media, 138-9
  limitations in time, 139
  dependence upon effect, 139
 what dramatist and minister have in difference, 139-141

DRAMA *(Cont.):*
  buildings, 139
  mood of audience, 140
  human and mechanical aids, 140-1
  methods, 141
 how the dramatist holds interest, 141-150
  character portrayal, 141
  analysis of Galsworthy's "Loyalties," 142-9
   story, 142
   character, 143
   motives, 144-5
  conflict, 146
  suspense, 146
  climax, 147
  emotion, 147
  spire of meaning, 148-9
  marketing a play, 149-150
 what the minister can learn from the dramatist, 150-8
  dramatic vs theatrical preaching, 151
  to think imaginatively, 152
  to present pictures and persons, 152-5
  to present struggle, 156
  to use suspense and climax, 157
 the conduct of a worship service, 159-167
  what total effect is desired?, 159-161
  importance of physical factors, 161-3
  progression of emotions, 164
  an ideal church service, 165-7

*Dramatic Works*
 Androcles, Shaw, 27
 Enemy of the People, Ibsen, 27
 Doll's House, Ibsen, 27
 Green Pastures, Connelly, 28
 Hamlet, Shakespeare, 148
 King Lear, Shakespeare, 148
 Loyalties, Galsworthy, 27, 142-9
 Our Town, Wilder, 28
 St. Joan, Shaw, 27
 Tobacco Road, Kirkland, 27